HALIFAX
CANADA'S SMART CITY

*The Board of Directors, Investors and Staff of the
Greater Halifax Partnership proudly dedicate this volume
to our community on its 250th Anniversary
1749-1999*

On behalf of the Halifax Regional Municipality, I am delighted to be a part of Halifax Canada's Smart City.

It is a wonderful time to be living and doing business in Greater Halifax. This volume is a photograph of our history and the unprecedented growth and opportunity in our community. Greater Halifax is one of Canada's heritage regions. It is the oldest city in English Canada and 1999 marks our 250th anniversary. The future looks very positive for our community, and as we celebrate our birthday, we are looking forward to exciting developments in Information Technology, Oil and Gas, Life Sciences and Transportation.

This volume is an indication of where we have been and where we are going. I hope everyone will enjoy this snapshot of Canada's Smart City.

Walter Fitzgerald
Mayor, Halifax Regional Municipality

HALIFAX
CANADA'S SMART CITY

By Ann Graham Walker
Edited by Brian Flemming
Corporate Profiles by Marilyn Pincock
Featuring the Photography of Jocelin d'Entremont

HALIFAX
CANADA'S SMART CITY

Produced in cooperation with
The Greater Halifax Partnership
1969 Upper Water Street
Halifax, Nova Scotia
Canada B3J 3R7

Text by Ann Graham Walker
Edited by Brian Flemming
Corporate Profiles by Marilyn Pincock
Featuring the Photography of Jocelin d'Entremont

Community Communications, Inc.
Publishers: Ronald P. Beers and James E. Turner
Publisher's Sales Associates: Stanley Blady and Gregory Thain
Acquisitions: Henry S. Beers
Executive Editor: James E. Turner
Senior Editor: Mary Shaw Hughes
Managing Editor: Bonnie Ashley Harris
Profile Editors: Kari Collin Jarnot and
Mary Catherine Richardson
Design Director: Scott Phillips
Designer: Ashley Margaret Wheeler
Production Artist: Ramona Davis
Photo Editors: Bonnie Ashley Harris and
Ashley Margaret Wheeler
Production Manager: Jarrod Stiff
Sales Assistant: Annette Lozier
Proofreaders: Wynona B. Hall and Kari Collin Jarnot
Accounting Services: Sara Ann Turner

C C I

Community Communications, Inc.
Montgomery, Alabama
James E. Turner, Chairman of the Board
Ronald P. Beers, President
Daniel S. Chambliss, Vice President

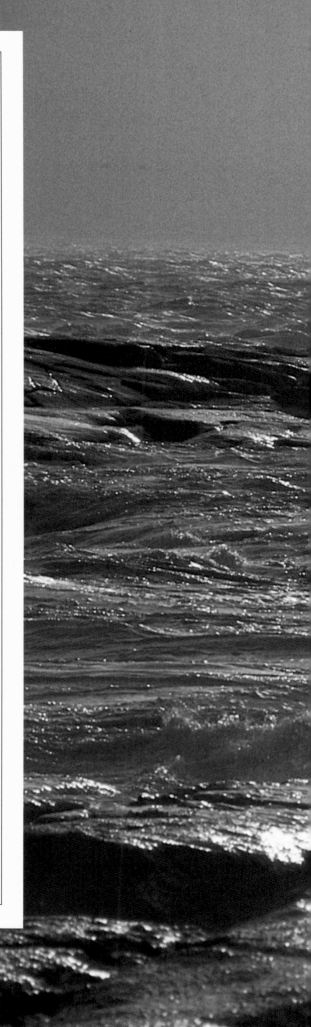

Halifax Public Gardens. Photo by Jocelin d'Entremont.

TABLE OF CONTENTS

PART I

THE MOST EXTRAORDINARY RESOURCE— HALIFAX'S INNOVATIVE PEOPLE

1

As a world trading and shipping crossroads for two hundred fifty years, Halifax has drawn resourceful immigrants from many nations. Its coastal location and pristine beauty are remarkable, but it is the *people* who are this city's prime resource.

PARADISE BY CONSENSUS—A SPECIAL PLACE TO LIVE

2

The people of Greater Halifax do not live here through casual circumstance. They live here by conviction. Halifax has a unique lifestyle which is cherished and protected by its citizens.

THE RIGHT CITY IN THE RIGHT PLACE AT THE RIGHT TIME

3

On the brink of a new millennium, Halifax is a city destined to prosper. It has the smartest labor force in Canada and a community of business leaders who believe strongly in the city's special advantages.

FORGING A TRAIL TO THE WORLD— THE NEW VIEW FROM THE CLASSROOM

4

Smart City—Halifax is at the head of the class with its array of educational facilities and talented and devoted educators and instructors. Halifax has more universities and colleges per capita than anywhere else in North America—energizing the city and bringing home a world of opportunities.

SOLID GOLD HEALTH CARE

5

People don't usually choose where they get sick. But if you could, you would do well to choose Halifax. Cutting edge research and world class medical facilities and health care institutes are identifying characteristics of Halifax's medical community.

FROM HERE TO ANYWHERE— HALIFAX'S GATEWAY ON THE WORLD

6

Halifax was created for trade and transport, a legacy which has shaped the city's history from the beginning. The shipping trade relies upon Halifax as a "first port in, last port out" for vessels in the Atlantic. Halifax's modern shipping terminals are linked to an efficient rail network, transcontinental roads and Canada's fastest growing international airport.

TITANIC—KEEPING WATCH ON THE ATLANTIC, A SPECIAL TRIBUTE

7

THE PEARL IN THE OYSTER—ARTS ALIVE

Halifax has a rich heritage and vast array of cultural and entertainment facilities, including a repertory theatre, a dance company, a symphony orchestra, four movie sound stages, an entertainment arena that holds ten thousand people, and an Imax theatre. And much more, making Halifax one of Canada's most vibrant art communities.

SMART CITY IN THE NEW MILLENNIUM

8

As Halifax sits poised on the threshold of a new millennium, the people of this unique city are celebrating its rich heritage and looking forward to a bright and optimistic future.

Lawrencetown Beach.

PART II

Photos on pages 4, 7, 8 and 10 by Jocelin d'Entremont.

FOREWORD

It had always looked like an old town. It had a genius for looking old and for acting as though nothing could possibly happen to surprise it.
Barometer Rising, Hugh MacLennan, 1941

Visitors to Halifax are often impressed by the city's striking blend of old and new. Our historic harbour is lined with modern office towers, ivy covered university buildings boast the latest in educational and research facilities, and heritage buildings house innovative technological and artistic ventures. It's sometimes taken for granted by those of us who live here, but it is this underlying sense of history, coupled with the excitement of new opportunities that make living and working in Halifax very special.

Halifax is Canada's **Smart City**. It is consistently ranked as one of the best places to do business in North America. A central location and magnificent harbour are just two of the city's advantages. Our proximity to newly discovered off-shore gas reserves, our integrated transportation network and extensive business services mean Halifax is a great port city, a new centre for off-shore oil and gas, emerging as North America's new energy capital. In addition, an independent study recently ranked Halifax as the best place in the world to do business in Life Sciences.

Six universities and an excellent community college system make our people the best educated in Canada. In today's fast-paced, digital world, the people of Halifax are a valuable resource for hundreds of smart companies such as Aliant, Keane, Cisco Systems, Mobil Oil, Nova Scotia Power, Silicon Graphics Inc., Royal Bank Group, and CGI Information Systems.

Halifax is also home to several leading research institutions, including the Bedford Institute of Oceanography, the Advanced Materials Engineering Centre, Telecom Applications Research Alliance, the QEII's Centre for Clinical Research, and the National Research Council Institute for Marine BioSciences. As the home base for Canada's Navy, Halifax is also the site of extensive research and development in the areas of aerospace and defense.

The Greater Halifax Partnership is the economic growth organization for our community. This independent private-public Partnership is unique in Canada. With investment from the public sector and from the city's business community, the Partnership is recognizable for marketing the **Smart City**, generating interest and developing external markets. Now recognized as the most successful economic development model in Canada, the Partnership is proud of its brief history which began with the amalgamation of four communities into one modern city.

Halifax is a top place to do business in North America because it's one of the best places to live. We enjoy the most temperate climate in Canada and celebrate our summers on magnificent beaches or sailing the coast. With some of the best restaurants in Canada, theatres, art galleries, a symphony orchestra and a diverse musical scene, Canada's oldest city has a vibrant young heart.

On behalf of the Board of Directors, Investors and Staff of the Greater Halifax Partnership, I hope you will enjoy *Halifax, Canada's Smart City* .

Michael MacDonald
President and CEO, Greater Halifax Partnership

PREFACE

This book begins with a chapter on people and ends in their own words. People lead the way in this city, keenly aware that the future is now. Smart, proactive, eager for the challenges of the 21st century, Halifax's people are what the city offers a world hungry for talent, ideas and a real sense of place—as you are about to discover.

Author's prefaces are always filled with thank yous. Now I know why. I want to make amends with my family for their patient restraint during the many months I spent at my computer, oblivious to the weeds in the garden and the dust bunnies under my feet. My husband, Joseph, deserves a medal for his careful reading of first drafts, as does Jocelyn Raymond, a writer and friend. Thank you to everyone who provided background information, especially Diane Marshall, Carly Casey, Lynn Ledwidge, John O'Brien, Stephen King, Chuck Bridges, Margaret Murphy and Hillary Cole.

To the people at the Greater Halifax Partnership who worked with me on this project—Brian Flemming, Michael MacDonald and Nancy Phillips, thank you for your helpful support. I also want to thank Bonnie Harris at Community Communications for her warm spirited guidance, professionalism and curiosity. To Jocelin d'Entremont—thank you for the beautiful photographs, the most important part of this book and for the hours you put in on the Angus L. Macdonald Bridge on a freezing winter's day getting just the right shot of the harbour.

And finally, to the people you will meet in these pages, thank you for your time, and for the part you play in making Halifax a lively and interesting place to live, work and do business.

Ann Graham Walker

PART I

Lake Banook. Photo by Jocelin d'Entremont.

CHAPTER 1

THE MOST EXTRAORDINARY RESOURCE—HALIFAX'S INNOVATIVE PEOPLE

(Above) The daughter and granddaughter of immigrants, Ruth Goldbloom has spent the past six years working for the restoration of Halifax's Pier 21—Canada's "Ellis Island." Pier 21 is Canada's last remaining immigrant shed. It has been preserved as a tribute to Canada's immigrant history and to the years between 1928 and 1971 during which approximately one-million immigrants arrived in Canada through Pier 21. Photo by Shannon Hannigar.

(Left) Halifax artist Terry MacDonald's painting of immigrants arriving at Pier 21.

Halifax—a dynamic city poised on Canada's Atlantic Shore. Ragged waves lash against timeless granite and a pine-covered island guards the entrance to one of the world's finest harbours. As a world trading and shipping crossroads for two hundred fifty years, Halifax has drawn resourceful immigrants from many nations. Its coastal location and pristine beauty are remarkable, but it is *people* who are this city's prime resource.

Smart, compact and charged with energy—Halifax is home to 340,000 individuals, a significant majority in their forties or younger. The city's brainy workforce has been widely heralded. Canada's national newspaper, *The Globe and Mail*, labeled Halifax one of Canada's "Smart Cities" in an article pointing out the city's exceptionally high ratio of knowledge workers and level of education.

Nearly sixty per cent of the labour force has a degree, diploma or certificate—twice the national average, in a country known for its high standards. The city has more PhDs per capita than just about anywhere in North America.

When Halifax stepped into the international spotlight in 1995, as host to the world's most powerful leaders during the G-7 Conference, many visitors were amazed to discover the city's wealth of resources. Television broadcasters referred to Halifax's "hip and lively" ambience. British Prime Minister John Major praised the city for what he called "the Friendly Summit." In a *Maclean's* magazine article, journalist John DeMont dubbed Halifax "the Last Best Place." Others simply called the city "Canada's best-kept secret."

Bedford Basin. Photo by Jocelin d'Entremont.

Eric Kitchen, president of Fastlane Technologies, a Newbridge affiliate, with some of his exceptional workforce atop Fastlane's downtown office in Halifax. Photo by Jocelin d'Entremont.

Today, word is spreading quickly. Halifax is a recognized centre of excellence in health care, biotechnology, pharmaceutical research, education and every aspect of the arts. In filmmaking—a local industry loaded with talent—revenues have increased tenfold in just five years. New Media, such as software and music production, are also taking off. Halifax's new oil and gas industry is adding to the city's bright profile. Initiated with the Sable Offshore Energy Project, vast natural gas reserves off the Nova Scotia coast are now being developed and further explored. Specialized professionals who are managing and servicing the development are concentrated in Halifax, and as the industry grows, so do the future possibilities.

Smart City workers—Eric Kitchen

Halifax is Canada's Smart City, and the corporate world is watching. A number of prestigious companies have chosen to establish bases in Halifax in recent years—companies such as Boston-based Keane Incorporated, Cisco Systems, and Newbridge Networks.

They come for many reasons—lifestyle, location, cost of doing business. High on the list are the exceptional work force and the broad range of educational facilities Halifax offers.

Eric Kitchen—in his late twenties and a native of Ontario—is president of Fastlane Technologies, a Newbridge affiliate that started up in Halifax in 1997. Kitchen has been in Halifax for a couple of years—long enough to appreciate the quality of the local workforce.

"What is special about the workers here is, not only are they smart and well-trained," he says, "they want to live here. That makes them more likely to be loyal to the company and to invest in its future. In this industry, those are rare qualities."

Kitchen wants to lure skilled Nova Scotians to his company. Fastlane has grown to a stage where he needs to attract management-level people with experience under their belt. Many of these sons and daughters moved to other centres during leaner times. Kitchen has used his web site—and national advertising in the *Globe and Mail*—to bring them home.

That is not to say his search is limited to "expatriate" Nova Scotians. Kitchen wants top-notch talent wherever it can be found. He takes prospective recruits on personal tours of the city, highlighting favourite features—Fastlane's central downtown office with its harbour view, the wealth of cultural events and bookstores, and the easy gatherings of friends that are so much a part of life here.

One of the city's best selling points, Kitchen enthuses, is its predilection for kindly courtesy. "You may find this strange but one of the first things I do when I bring someone here is get them to step out on the street at a crosswalk. Even on a busy intersection, the trucks, cars, motorcycles all come to a stop."

"I don't think people here realize just how amazing that is."

Trying what has not been tried before—Andrew Cochran

At the waterfront edge in the city centre, a pair of high-rise buildings known as Purdy's Wharf look down the length of the harbour to the open Atlantic. It is a dramatic vista—the play of light on the water, the tugboats, the ships and ferries passing back and forth and McNab's Island, rich in history, signaling the harbour's entrance. There is a sense of the world on your doorstep, within touching distance.

THE BEDFORD INSTITUTE OF OCEANOGRAPHY

The Bedford Institute of Oceanography is located on the shores of Halifax Harbour and is Canada's largest centre for ocean research. The first major federal centre devoted to oceanography, the Bedford Institute has grown to rank among the most respected ocean research institutions in the world. Its scientists and research facilities are a major source of inspiration and support for companies and institutions which need ocean knowledge in their business.

The Institute and the scientific teams represented there have three goals—to create Canadian centres of excellence in scientific research and the advancement and dissemination of knowledge, to better apply this scientific knowledge in achieving Canada's economic and social goals and to contribute to a better quality of life for all Canadians. ·❖·

CHAPTER 3

THE RIGHT CITY IN THE RIGHT PLACE AT THE RIGHT TIME— HALIFAX'S TALENT-BASED ECONOMY

(Above) Michael MacDonald, President and CEO of the Greater Halifax Partnership. Photo by Jocelin d'Entremont.

(Left) Halifax is one of the most exciting cities in North America today. Photo by Jocelin d'Entremont.

The "Smart City" Advantage

On the brink of a new millennium, the cities destined to prosper are those with the imagination to produce good ideas, the knowledge required to build innovative solutions and the audacity to take on the world.

Halifax is the right city in the right place at the right time. Halifax has the smartest labor force in Canada, the highest per capita concentration of universities in North America and a community of business leaders who believe strongly in the city's unique advantages.

In Halifax, the knowledge economy is well advanced. The shift from a manufacturing and resource-based society has been taking place over a period of several decades. Sixty-seven percent of the area's jobs are in service and knowledge-related occupations.

Seventy per cent of Halifax's population is under the age of 44. The labor force participation rate is one of the highest in Canada, second only to oil-rich Alberta. Halifax's rate of capital investment *is* the highest in Canada, with the dynamic growth of the city's Post-Panamax container port and massive new oil and gas developments poised to inject further investment.

Sable Offshore Energy Inc.—SOEI—a $3 billion project off the Nova Scotia coast which will bring gas to the maritimes and U.S. Northeast is just the tip of the iceburg. The projected impact on Halifax is already being compared to the transformation of Aberdeen, Scotland, after the discovery of North Sea oil.

The initial phase of this project is developing natural gas reserves of more than three trillion cubic feet. The full extent of the reserve is more than five times what is currently under development. Oil and gas industry experts predict Sable Island will inject vast revenues into the Nova Scotia economy and provide clean, economical power.

"The Sable Offshore Energy project is just the beginning," says SOEI President and General Manager John Brannan. "There are many other leases and blocks of land out there that are currently owned by other operators. They are watching this project very closely."

Halifax is one of the most exciting cities in North America today. You can point to example after example—people setting ambitious goals for themselves and their community, and then surpassing

---

The dynamic growth of Halifax's post-panamax container port is a key factor in the city's economic growth and stability. Shipping experts are keenly aware that Halifax's deepwater channel puts the city in an ideal position to serve Post-Panamax vessels, ships too large to navigate the Panama Canal. Photo by Jocelin d'Entremont.

them. This is a city that is taking charge of its own future and has done so with energy and vision.

Smart growth

Halifax is the hub of Eastern Canada, particularly with respect to service, knowledge and transportation industries. Financial service businesses have regional offices here. So do a broad range of consulting firms that do business internationally. The Sable Offshore Energy project will expand this sector dramatically.

As the capital of Nova Scotia, many government offices are located in Halifax such as the Atlantic Canada Opportunities Agency, the National Film Board and the Canadian Broadcasting Corporation. The provincial legislature and most government agencies are here, giving people easy access to decision-makers.

Halifax attracts more international air and sea traffic than any other Atlantic Canadian city. The move towards Post-Panamax container vessels will increase this traffic further, because no other East Coast city north of Virginia has the channel depth to handle these ships without costly dredging.

Teaching and training, developing new foods from biological sources, creating software applications, writing and producing material for international broadcast, designing better ways for governments to deliver services, travelling and trading, caring for the sick. These are the type of activities that set the city's pulse. They are environmentally friendly, mobile, exportable, ideally suited for development and growth—and they account for 90 per cent of Halifax's *new* jobs over the past decade.

Some of Halifax's emerging industries achieved international prominence so quickly that locals are still walking around pinching themselves. In the film industry, for example, annual revenues have increased tenfold in the past five years, and now exceed $100 million.

Halifax's Salter Street Films is a good example of what happens when you combine good ideas, professional skills and entrepreneurial vision. Building on the artistic integrity of its two founding brothers—Paul and Michael Donovan—the company has a long list of prestigious awards and a slew of successful national and international television productions, including *Lexx, the Dark Zone, This Hour Has 22 Minutes* and *Emily of New Moon.*

Now Salter Street is pioneering a new frontier in the world of entertainment—by developing interactive products that can be beamed into people's homes via the Internet.

"We see the Internet as another broadcast medium," says Michael Heller, one of the driving forces behind Salter Street New Media. "It is one that is growing rapidly and does not have dominant players the way the television industry does, for example. With new media such as the Internet, the opportunities for creating the best content are wide open."

Salter Street is not the only Halifax company that is establishing an international reputation in New Media. The city's rich nucleus of

Saipen S-7000 crane in the Halifax Harbour. Photo by Jocelin d'Entremont.

universities has produced a young and vibrant information technology sector, with revenue growth of 30 per cent a year.

Cities everywhere are rushing to build a base in information technology and New Media but, like a figure skater with a cache of winning moves, Halifax has the potential to stand out. The city gets high marks in both artistic vision and technical know-how—with creative resources like The Nova Scotia College of Art and Design actively participating in the development of New Media technologies, together with Halifax's five other universities, the private sector and government.

Halifax is, indeed, a "Smart City"—with an energy level that is *positively magnetic.* The Greater Halifax Partnership logos that say this are bang on. High levels of education and technology run through every sector like a ribbon. In today's economy, that is equivalent to sitting on a mother lode—except it is better. Knowledge is a renewable resource.

Targeting the winners

If you ask people in this city to name Halifax's most promising and dynamic sector they will all give you the same answer: arts and entertainment. And they are right.

Halifax's burgeoning creative industries are a major force in the local economy. The city has a distinct culture that is deeply rooted in Nova Scotia's long history and rich narrative traditions.

Halifax is also becoming a centre of growth and excellence in other exciting areas—such as environmental technologies, marine sciences and the development of value-added products from agriculture and natural resources.

Dr. Ross McCurdy is the chief executive officer of Innovacorp—a corporation established by the province to act as a kind of "midwife" in the development of promising, technology- rich sectors. Innovacorp has targeted knowledge technology and life sciences as bright lights in the Halifax economy, with a special emphasis on marine sciences.

Marine sciences are being fostered because of the city's coastal location and the long-term implications of the Sable Offshore Energy project. Dr. McCurdy also speaks glowingly of Halifax's potential in the life sciences-biotechnical medical devices and health-related technologies."

"We believe that Nova Scotia is just blessed with a lot of assets," Dr. McCurdy says, flipping through a set of overheads that describe Innovacorp's work with the technology sector. "We have a leading Canadian medical school. The Queen Elizabeth II Health Sciences Centre is the fourth largest in the country—just loaded with expertise. If we look at the government research organizations that are located here, there is the National Research Council on Oxford Street. There is the Bedford Institute of Oceanography—world renowned in marine sciences. There are first-class Health Canada labs in the city."

Recently 185 Nova Scotia companies involved in life sciences joined together in a partnership, with the goal of doubling the industry within the next three years. "I don't think we are going to

The Electropolis Sound Stage is one of four movie sound stages in the
Greater Halifax area. Photo by Jocelin d'Entremont.

have any difficulty reaching those targets," says Dr. McCurdy. "We're
going to do even *better*."

A focus on exports

Halifax is taking on the world—as it has previously in its two-hun-
dred-and-fifty years of history. The city is marketing education and
brainpower at a rate that is outpacing the methodology of statisticians.

Nova Scotia's foreign exports are calculated to have increased by 30
per cent in recent years. That figure does not include knowledge-based
projects—such as the Kuwait-Dalhousie Rehabilitation Project, Dr.
Lydia Makrides' training program for physiotherapists in Kuwait; or
Dorothy Spence and Linda Weaver's marketing of "TeleHealth"; or
Hector Jacques's successful export of environmental consulting services
to countries around the world or the regular appearance of Andrew
Cochran's *Theodore Tugboat* on international television. Talent-based
commodities such as these are difficult to track as they enter and leave
a country, because tracking methods still deal in terms of physical
goods and cargo containers.

Many of the knowledge-based products Halifax are exporting are
on the leading edge. Dalhousie University's new Master of
Engineering in Internetworking—the only program of its kind in
the world—will soon be exported to several countries through a
process of real-time, multi-media video conferencing. This is a
dynamic technology that can take a Halifax-based virtual classroom
anywhere, with active participation by students in each location. The

project is underway at Halifax's Telecom Applications Research
Alliance (TARA) laboratories.

The Masters of Engineering in Internetworking distance education
project is a partnership between TARA, Cisco Systems, Dalhousie
University and Maritime Tel&Tel (MTT).

Another innovative knowledge-export venture is Nova Health
International's marketing of Halifax's medical expertise, through a
project that combines entrepreneurial and humanitarian objectives.
Nova Health International (NHI) is a corporation affiliated with the
Dean's Office at Dalhousie Medical School. NHI is using Nova
Scotia's TeleHealth technology to market medical expertise in places
where it would not otherwise be accessible. X-rays taken on the
Caribbean island of St. Kitts-Nevis are read by radiologists at the
Queen Elizabeth II Health Sciences Centre within twenty-four
hours. The program is generating $3 million worth of revenues for
the medical school. There are plans to expand the model to other
islands, perhaps also to cruise ships.

On home ground in Halifax, NHI has become an enabler for medical research. Internationally, it is helping to support other projects,
such as an international forum on medical ethics. NHI's director, Dr.
Ron Stewart, is passionate about balancing humanitarian and entrepreneurial objectives.

Dr. Stewart is a world expert on emergency medicine. He is a
former medical director of paramedic training for the County of Los
Angeles and established the Center for Emergency Medicine at the
University of Pittsburgh. Dr. Stewart is also a former Nova Scotia
health minister and a leading figure in Canada's drive to conclude an
international land mines treaty.

Dr. Kenneth Ozmon, President, Saint Mary's University, community leader, and a member of the Board of Directors of Greater Halifax Partnership, is the longest serving University President in Canada. Photo by Jocelin d'Entremont.

"My idea of a sound infrastructure in international affairs includes this educational and humanitarian component," says Dr. Stewart. "It is a longstanding business practice to be involved in the community in a charitable way. If you are serious about working in the international arena, you have to be serious about humanitarian programs."

Saint Mary's University President, Dr. Ken Ozmon, shares Dr. Stewart's commitment to internationalism. Dr. Ozmon has initiated many international exchanges and development projects during his twenty-year tenure. He began marketing his university's programs in countries like Indonesia long before knowledge-export became fashionable.

"We are turning out people with a broader vision of the world," he says. "It's not just about Halifax. It is about Halifax, plus Brussels, plus Rio, and so on. When you see yourself as capable of dancing on the international stage, you don't have any restriction on where you can market your product—whether your product is yourself as a consultant or whether it is the goods that you are manufacturing."

A stone's throw from world markets

Two of the world's most powerful economic unions—the European Economic Community and the North American Free Trade Zone—are on Halifax's doorstep, easily connected by sea. These are Halifax's natural and traditional trade corridors.

Halifax is closer to Boston than it is to Montreal. New York is closer than Toronto. The travel time by sea to Europe is a full day's sailing closer than from any other major North American port. The

The growth and success of Halifax's new media sector is being driven by the city's talented youth. Bill McMullin is the CEO of InfoInterActive Telcom—a company that has developed a program that manages incoming calls when your phone line is tied up on the Internet. InfoInter Active designed the technology using the DMS-100 switch that is available at the TARA research laboratory. Photo by Jocelin d'Entremont.

city's prime trade location is being marketed worldwide.

The Greater Halifax Partnership was instrumental in forming the Canadian Swedish Businesses Association, recognizing that Sweden is Nova Scotia's biggest foreign investor. In 1997 alone, Swedish business injected $1.5 billion into the province's economy. Atlantic Container Lines has its Canadian headquarters here. Another Swedish-owned corporation—Stora Forest Industries—recently completed a $750-million expansion of its Nova Scotia pulp and paper manufacturing plant.

In June of 1998, a trade delegation of fifty Halifax businesses traveled to Sweden. They visited Stockholm and Goteborg and laid the groundwork for valuable new business between the two communities. The Partnership is successfully marketing Halifax as a strategic gateway to NAFTA—while the city's European partners offer an entry point to the European Economic Community.

If geography is proving to be an advantage, Halifax's digitalized fiber-optic telecommunications network brings the world even closer. "Twenty minutes to the beach and two minutes to Tokyo" as a federal cabinet minister put it on a recent visit to the city. Halifax is in a

Nova Health International Director Dr. Ron Stewart is a world expert on emergency medicine. Photo by Jocelin d'Entremont.

enhancement to Halifax's promising pharmaceutical industry.

In example after example, the cost of doing business here is the most competitive in North America, according to a recent KPMG study that looked at 64 cities of comparable size. The study looked at eight key industries, including electronics, pharmaceuticals, telecommunications and software production.

Factors such as these are drawing new investment to the area—from Newbridge affiliate companies like Fastlane Technologies to the Bank of Nova Scotia call centre, and clinical trials which have shown an 80 per cent investment growth in recent years.

Local companies are growing as well. When the Halifax marketing consultant Steve Stairs first began working for CorporaTel—a telecommunications firm that specializes in call centres—"there were about 250 people working for CorporaTel and the seven other companies affiliated with its parent company, Corporate Communications Limited."

"Now there are over six hundred employees," Stairs says. The numbers have doubled over the past ten months. He expects them to triple in the next couple of years.

A recent survey by the Greater Halifax Partnership polled its members to gauge their degree of optimism about the economy. Eighty-

Joanne Jellet of Jellet Bioteck. Jellet has developed diagnostic test kits for the maritime industry. Photo by Jocelin d'Entremont.

position to take advantage of this opportunity. The level of Internet usage here is one of the highest in the world.

Still on the subject of location—Halifax enjoys a time zone that is ideal for trade. Film producer Chris Zimmer can sit in his offices in Burnside Industrial Park and talk to colleagues in Los Angeles or Frankfurt, all in the course of a working day.

Zimmer's company Imagex has produced a number of feature films with European partners, including *Margaret's Museum* and *Love and Death in Long Island*. The latter was on the *Time* magazine's list of ten best films in 1997, and it won the Best First Feature award at the Cannes Film Festival in the same year.

Zimmer has no difficulty attracting British, Dutch and German partners because he is well respected in the industry—and because the Nova Scotia government's film tax credits are grabbing people's attention. The government introduced the incentives in 1994, just as the industry was taking off. It is a fully refundable corporate tax credit which rebates producers 32.5 per cent of the cost of the Nova Scotia labor expenditures employed in a production, or 16.25 per cent of a film's total budget. Every tax-credit dollar is tied to a Nova Scotia job.

These tax credits are specially earmarked for the film industry, but other sectors share in Halifax's favorable environment. The government offers attractive incentives for research and development—an

Halifax developer John Lindsay, Jr. manages Purdy's Wharf, one of the city's flagship real estate developments. Photo by Jocelin d'Entremont.

seven per cent rated Halifax favorably as a location for business—because of its proximity to markets, its business connections and its quality of life. Companies are developing new products and new markets, investing in new facilities and making optimistic projections. As for their satisfaction with the local workforce, more than 90 per cent of those polled gave their employees high ratings for reliability, productivity and attitude.

"We have the potential for having an economy that is so good, so diversified and positioned so much in the right way, it's almost scary!" says John Lindsay, Jr., a Halifax developer who manages Purdy's Wharf on the city's waterfront. Purdy's Wharf—a pair of sleek towers that evoke unfurling sails—is one of the city's flagship real estate developments. It has made a mark both nationally and internationally for its indoor air quality, its innovative engineering solutions and its workplace enhancement issues, such as the provision of high-standard daycare on site. Lindsay is wildly enthusiastic about the diverse range of opportunities on the city's doorstep. He compares the current climate to Halifax's boom years during the 1850s, 60s and 70s, when the city prospered on banking, global trade and, yes—privateering.

"We come from *pirates*," Lindsay laughs. "We made a whole pile of money going out and plundering. Now it is time to be just as fearless about the trade opportunities that are out there—not only in the States but also around the world!

There are big pictures here. Big, *big* pictures." ❖

Point Pleasant Park. Photo by Jocelin d'Entremont.

CHAPTER 4

FORGING A TRAIL TO THE WORLD— THE VIEW FROM THE CLASSROOM

(Above) Opportunities abound for Halifax's youth to participate in sports. Photo by Jocelin d'Entremont.

(Left) Dalhousie University, Halifax's largest, was the first non-sectarian university in British North America. It was founded in 1818 by Lord Dalhousie. Photo by Jocelin d'Entremont.

A City of Students

Halifax is a "university town". The city has six highly respected universities and a steady population of thirty thousand students. Five thousand university employees contribute to the city's knowledge base. In today's economy, that is like sitting on a gold mine.

Not all learning takes place in the classroom. These elementary school students have read about Joseph Howe in their history books but an excursion to Province House is even better. This statue of Howe is a few yards away from the spot where in 1835, as a young newspaper publisher, he successfully defended himself against a charge of criminal libel. His acquittal established the principle of freedom of the press in Canada. Howe went on to become a prominent Nova Scotia politician. The building next to Howe is Province House. This building is recognized as a perfect Adams-style building, and is the oldest legislature outside of Britain. Photo by Jocelin d'Entremont.

People come from all over the world to study here. There is no shortage of options. Dalhousie University grants professional degrees in Law, Engineering, Architecture, Dentistry, Medicine and Allied Health Professions, as well as doctoral degrees in a broad variety of areas. The University of King's College offers a degree in Journalism. The Atlantic School of Theology is a multi-denominational institution that trains men and women for the ministry. Mount Saint Vincent University has a degree program in Public Relations and a strong focus on Distance Education. At Saint Mary's University the Frank H. Sobey Faculty of Commerce prepares students for the international world of business—with a recently added doctoral program.

Halifax is home to the Nova Scotia College of Art and Design (NSCAD). A top-ranking art and design school, NSCAD is helping to position Halifax as a centre for innovative New Media development. The Nova Scotia Community College is also a strategic asset, with three Halifax campuses and a technology-rich curriculum.

The city's cluster of universities is a lively cultural and international resource. They each have art galleries, visiting professors, live music concerts, continuing education programs and top-notch libraries. The University of King's College has an unusual collection of rare books.

Dalhousie University has a performance auditorium that is enjoyed by the entire community. The Saint Mary's University "Huskies"—a football team—have fans around the world, thanks to the university's high ratio of international students.

Even off-campus, the universities energize this city with youth and discourse. Commuters tune into multicultural programs on CKDU, the Dalhousie University radio station. Coffee shops on Spring Garden Road are abuzz with conversation. Young people carrying backpacks and medical students wearing pagers hurry along the streets. If you wander into an "alternative" video store like "Critics Choice"—run by a former NSCAD student—the notes and flyers pinned on the bulletin board tell a story all their own. A foreign student willing to give Spanish lessons. A benefit for a Philippine refugee. A free concert by T-shirted musicians promoting their first CD. A live jazz performance at the Café Mokka. A one-way ticket to Toronto selling cheap. And so on . . . .

Economic driver

Halifax is smart, hip and youthful, and the universities are a big part of the picture. They also drive "the Big Picture": the growth of the knowledge-based economy.

When the Boston-based software company Keane Inc. decided to locate its first Canadian plant in Halifax, people asked how they made their choice. Very easy, was the answer. Halifax has a skilled work force with a level of education and a training infrastructure that cannot be matched anywhere else in Canada.

Another well-known company, Cisco Systems, paid a similar tribute a few months later, when they announced they were coming to Halifax. Cisco—the largest internetworking company in the world—made its statement before a distinguished audience at the Softworld '96 Conference, held in Halifax that year. The Technical University of Nova Scotia (now merged with Dalhousie University) had been alma mater to many of Cisco's best employees. Establishing a branch office in Halifax would bring those resources closer.

Within its first year in Halifax, Cisco became a key partner in Halifax's Telecom Applications Research Alliance (TARA)—a research and testing facility for innovative telecommunications-based technologies. Cisco established a Cisco certification laboratory in the TARA facilities—one of five such laboratories in the world—and equipped the laboratory with a DMS-100 telecommunications switch. New technologies such as Dorothy Spence and Linda Weaver's TeleHealth network have been tested and developed in the TARA labs, using the DMS-100 switch—available to TARA members.

Cisco has now partnered with Dalhousie University and Maritime Tel & Tel (MTT) to develop a Master of Engineering in Internetworking, which we learned about earlier in this book. The program is unique in the world, fine-tuned to industry needs. And Dalhousie is involved in a number of other important projects with Cisco—piloting new technologies, giving the company feedback.

Dave McIlveen is Cisco's branch manager for Atlantic Canada. Around forty years young, and enthusiastic about Halifax, McIlveen says his company's relationship with the city's universities and corporate communities has been crucial.

"There are not too many places in the world where you can get this level of co-operation from people in the community," he says.

Going that extra mile

The Cisco story shows how Halifax's high-octane cluster of universities is helping to create new opportunities. Halifax also has a number of private-sector facilities including McKenzie College and the Information Technology Institute (ITI). These schools are working closely with industry and turning out job-ready students well trained in a variety of IT and New Media skills. McKenzie College and ITI have been so successful here on home ground that they have begun expanding. ITI has facilities in many locations including Moncton, Ottawa, Toronto, Vancouver, Calgary and Denver, Colorado.

The Nova Scotia Community College (NSCC) is also a valuable resource, particularly in a "Smart City" like this where people embrace the idea of learning and re-training. Four years ago NSCC had two hundred students enrolled in continuing education programs in Halifax. Now—with some new courses in areas like computer and communications skills—enrollment has climbed to 5,000.

The Community College's "customized training" program is also getting high marks with a growing list of private sector clients, including the Bank of Nova Scotia (Scotiabank). NSCC's customized training proposal influenced Scotiabank's decision to set up a call centre in Halifax, bringing 166 high-end call centre jobs to the city.

Allister Thorne—Principal of NSCC's Halifax Campuses—believes teamwork developed between the College and Scotiabank set a valuable precedent. "It wasn't like someone came knocking on the door and said we'd like to buy a fifty-hour course in Windows, or something ready-made like that," he explains. "We worked very closely with the company to understand the company's culture, the company's requirements and needs. We designed our classrooms to mirror the facilities people would be using at their own site."

"Once the people were trained, we went down to the floor to help them make the transition to actual working conditions, and then got feedback from the company to see how we could improve things along the way."

Jack Keith is Scotiabank's Senior Vice President. He thinks the initiative's success has set a new standard across the country.

"Bankers are not people to gush," he admits, "but we are very, very pleased with the way the Community College has fulfilled all of our needs. I think it will bring other companies to this area."

Denis Leclaire, director of International Activities at St. Mary's and pictured here with some of the international students and faculty, is committed to what he calls the "internationalization" of today's universities. Photo by Jocelin d'Entremont.

Scotiabank's Pierrette Barrie—who worked closely on the project—has even stronger words of praise.

"I'll tell you from the bottom of my heart, there is no doubt in my mind that the Community College here and Nova Scotia have put their leadership and their name on something they can take right across the country as number one."

Beyond the "ivory tower"

Academic traditions run deep in Halifax. The University of Kings' College is the oldest in Canada—more than two hundred years old, with roots that reach across the United States border. The founders of King's were Anglican loyalists who had previously established a university in New York City (later renamed Columbia). Dalhousie University, Halifax's largest, was the first non-sectarian university in British North America. Dalhousie lays claim to many notable alumnae, from Lucy Maud Montgomery of *Anne of Green Gables* fame to ten provincial premiers. Mount Saint Vincent started in 1873 as an Academy run by the Sisters of Charity. It began granting degrees in 1925, Canada's only women's university. (MSVU is now co-educational). Halifax's Irish Catholic community founded Saint Mary's University in 1802—a primarily undergraduate institution that now boasts the region's only PhD program in Commerce.

These distinct origins give each institution a unique personality and culture. But their attachment to the past ends right about there. Halifax universities have their windows wide open to the world.

Government sources of funding are diminishing and Halifax's universities cannot afford to be "ivory towers." New partnerships

with industry are enhancing university infrastructure and forging closer links with the community. Academic researchers have developed a new fluency with so-called "technology transfer"—turning good research ideas into innovative products and solutions.

A research powerhouse for the region, Dalhousie University attracts more than $41 million in externally sponsored funding each year. Dalhousie has nine industrial Chairs involving corporate sponsorship. For example, the 3M Corporation-funded professorship for basic research in physics is currently involved in advanced battery research.

International traffic zone

Research partnerships are not the only sign that Halifax universities are changing. They are becoming entrepreneurial, marketing their knowledge and established links with the international community.

Scotiabank's Pierrette Barrie worked very closely with Nova Scotia Community College's "customized training" program. Photo by Trena Biddington.

The University of King's College, founded in 1789, is the oldest chartered university in Canada. Photo by Jocelin d'Entremont.

NSCAD draws students from seventeen different countries. Mount Saint Vincent University is selling Distance Education in the global market. Dalhousie University has development projects worth $80 million in a broad variety of regions, including Africa, Asia, Latin America, the Caribbean and Central and Eastern Europe. Dalhousie's School of Physiotherapy is developing physiotherapy facilities in Kuwait. Nova Health International is marketing Dalhousie's medical expertise all over the world.

Saint Mary's University (SMU) is also very active internationally. SMU is granting Bachelor of Arts degrees in the Gambia region of Africa. SMU's goal is to help the people of Gambia establish a fully accredited university of their own—the University of Gambia. Saint Mary's is also providing customized Executive MBA programs to corporate executives in China.

Denis Leclaire is the Director of International Activities at SMU. He has been involved in international education since the early seventies. He is committed to what he calls the "internationalization" of today's universities.

"It's about more than just having foreign students on campus," says Leclaire emphatically. "It is the creation of international traffic—which means that universities in Halifax are involved in technical assistance projects; they're involved in contract education internationally; they're involved in ensuring that there is a level of intelligence relating to international issues.

I am not going to deny that the kind of initiatives we are involved in bring in money, but the payback goes beyond direct financial returns. The payback comes in allowing students to have some type of experience with people from other cultures, so that they can function in an international context and gain a real awareness of the world outside." ⚬

CHAPTER
5

SOLID GOLD
HEALTH CARE

(Above) Medical students at Dalhousie University have been helping to develop a technology that could revolutionize the way the students of the future hone their techniques. "The Phantom" is a simulator first developed at the Massachusetts Institute of Technology as a training tool for engineers and aircraft technicians. Now the Dalhousie Medical School is working in partnership with Digital-Image FX, a Halifax software company, to develop medical applications. When the technology is fully developed, students will be able to use it to practice surgical techniques. Photo courtesy of Digital Image FX.

(Left) Newborns, along with their mothers, find themselves in very good and caring hands in Halifax. Seen here is Tanya Rafter with baby Lindsay MacKay. Photo by Jocelin d'Entremont.

People don't usually choose where they get sick. But if you could, you would do well to choose Halifax.

Halifax is a major tertiary-care referral center, with high-quality consultants and hospital services and a track record of groundbreaking research. It is also a respected health care training centre, drawing students from around the world. Within a few blocks of one another, in the heart of the city, you will find a cluster of first-class hospitals alongside Dalhousie University's superb medical, dental, pharmaceutical, physiotherapy and nursing schools. Health care professionals come here to pursue knowledge at every stage of their career.

As part of the province's public health care system, emergency health care providers in Halifax are always prepared. Photo by Jocelin d'Entremont.

An extraordinarily high concentration of talent—Dr. Howard Dickson

High caliber medical care and research facilities are more than a quality of life issue. They are the intellectual capital that draws talent from around the world, enriching Halifax's "Smart City" resources. Dr. Howard Dickson is a Professor of Anatomy and Neurobiology at Halifax's Dalhousie University and a former Associate Dean of Research and Planning at the university's Medical School. As one of Dalhousie's key recruiters, he is in a good position to observe just what it is that brings people here—or, for that matter, what motivates his own commitment to the area. Dr. Dickson is a native of Ontario who has lived and worked in Halifax for more than twenty years.

There are many factors that make Halifax compelling as a place to live—but Dr. Dickson identifies two which stand out for his recruits. People are impressed by "the intellectual capacity of the institution (Dalhousie University) and the willingness of people to collaborate," he says. "That's a very powerful statement for others to perceive on a short visit—so, yes, we do have a very collaborative spirit and there is a willingness to look beyond the traditional academic bounds and reach out . . . either across departments or across disciplines.

Dr. and Mrs. Howard Dickson. Dr. Dickson, Professor of Anatomy and Neurobiology at Halifax's Dalhousie University, is a Associate Vice President, Research and International Relations. Photo by Jocelin d'Entremont.

As an added bonus, I think the lifestyle here plays a huge role," Dr. Dickson continues. "Housing is relatively affordable. It's a wonderful place to raise a family . . . and if you compare us to Toronto or Vancouver, I don't know how they can recruit people to go to those places, especially young people. You are doomed to live in an apartment maybe forty-five minutes to an hour and a half away from the university, whereas it's very affordable here in Halifax."

The community's collaborative and focused approach to doing things works to attract—and keep—new talent. It has also produced some major successes for this area. "We clearly have at Dalhousie one of the best neuroscience communities in the world . . . I don't think there's any question about either the quality of the individuals or their contributions to the science," says Dr. Dickson. Other leading research areas are in cardiovascular research, cancer immunology, infectious diseases and clinical trials.

In recent years the World Health Care Organization has selected Halifax as the venue for a number of key health care planning forums. One such gathering was the Intersectoral Action for Health conference in 1997—an event that drew participants from twenty-five countries to endorse a new global health policy. While the agenda was international in scope, it was also an opportunity to showcase some of the important work being done in Halifax.

Tackling a killer disease—Dr. Jafna Cox

Dr. Jafna Cox, a research cardiologist, is on the front line of a particularly high-profile initiative. He is the driving force behind the "ICONS" study (Improving Cardiovascular Outcomes in Nova Scotia)—one of the largest population-based studies of heart disease ever undertaken. ICONS is closely following a large group of patients over a five-year period. It monitors the effect of lifestyle, information and particular treatments, gathering evidence and identifying the measures that result in clear improvement for patients. The study is also unique in its consultative approach. Everyone who has a stake in ICONS—from patients to private sector corporations to health advocacy groups—has an opportunity to participate and give feedback. It is an experiment in what Dr. Cox calls "evidence-based health care reform."

Dr. Jafna Cox, a research cardiologist, is the driving force behind the"ICONS" study (Improving Cardiovascular Outcomes in Nova Scotia)—one of the largest population-based studies of heart disease ever undertaken. Photo by Jocelin d'Entremont.

Dr. Cox praises the area as "an ideal laboratory" for an ambitious project such as ICONS—geographically small and easy to get around, yet large enough to make statistical results significant. There is a single province-wide health care system, so it is easy to share and gather data. Better still, there is that friendly spirit we keep hearing about, which enables people to work together on a challenging project such as ICONS. This is what Dr. Cox loves best about living and working in Halifax. "I talk to colleagues from other parts of the country," he says, "and that's the one part they can't figure . . . how you can get seventy people into a room (patients, nurses, advocacy groups, funding partners from the private sector, government, hospital administrators, etc.)—and everyone does not start squawking!"

Dr. Cox is a bright and ambitious young man who likes to set himself large challenges. He designed the ICONS project, persuaded a drug company (Merck Frosst) to fund it and got the support of the city's largest hospital and the Nova Scotia government. His brave and idealistic approach to knowledge gathering is extraordinary. But he is not the only member of Halifax's health care community who is venturing into new territory.

Exporting Halifax Brainpower—Dr. Lydia Makrides

A couple of blocks from the ICONS headquarters in the Queen Elizabeth II Health Sciences Centre lies the rambling, Victorian neighborhood of Dalhousie University. This is a particularly gracious quarter of town. Banks of large shade trees flank the streets—including lindens, elms and maples. Charming old houses sit alongside several generations of classroom buildings. Students crowd the sidewalks, back and forth from class.

Dr. Lydia Makrides directs the university's school of physiotherapy. She is also the mover and shaker behind the $30-million Kuwait-Dalhousie Rehabilitation Project—the largest contract ever awarded to a university-based health care project in Canada. The project has placed forty-two Canadians in Kuwait, ranging from physiotherapists to allied health professionals and support staff. They are teaching, training and delivering health care services. They are developing an independent Kuwaiti physiotherapy and rehabilitation unit—and learning to navigate the global economy.

Dr. Makrides is a Greek Cypriot who has lived in Halifax for more than twenty years. She has seen a lot of the world and was quick to recognize the potential when the Kuwaiti government invited her to submit a proposal to train physiotherapists in their country. "We have a knowledge-based economy, and marketing this knowledge is very lucrative," she points out, with enthusiasm. "First of all, it is culturally enriching for the Canadians who are there . . . they learn from that environment. They also come back to their own environment and realize how good things are here. It is also professionally enriching."

The Kuwait project has been a resounding success. Unlike many similar projects, its objective from the beginning was to set up a facility that would stand on its own. The focus has been on transferring the skills and expertise that enable Kuwaitis to deliver physiotherapy and rehabilitation services according to the highest Canadian standards. Dr. Makrides says that approach has been so well received, it has brought home a host of new opportunities—opportunities which foster internationalism, and which provide the university with a welcome infusion of cash.

"Universities are moving away from their traditional role of teaching in the classroom," Dr. Makrides says. "Now we are taking the university out . . . we are exploring, networking, taking the classroom out globally. There is no reason why we can't do that!"

Interestingly enough, it was a contact made through a foreign student that led to the Kuwait project. Halifax universities draw thousands of students from all over the world. That translates into a valuable networking resource, both today and for the future. The Kuwaiti project alone has created 240 direct and indirect full-time jobs and a significant infusion of capital into the local economy.

Pushing the boundaries of knowledge

Canadians have long known that Halifax is one of the country's finest hospital and medical treatment, research and training centres. Initiatives like the ICONS study and the Kuwait-Dalhousie project demonstrate that it is also one of the most innovative.

The recent announcement of six new fully funded Research Chairs in medicine can only enhance the city's position as a centre of excellence. Twelve million dollars in private endowments have created the Kathryn Allen Weldon Chair in Alzheimer's research, the Joan and Jack Craig Chair in autism, the Dr. Paul Janssen Research Chair in psychotic disorders at the Nova Scotia Hospital, a Chair in ophthalmology research which will focus on glaucoma and diseases of the retina, a Chair in surgery research and a Chair in internal medicine research which will concentrate on non-surgical treatment areas. A recent British study ranks Canada's medical technology and practice as second only to Sweden. Halifax's solid gold health care is on the leading edge locally and nationally—and, increasingly, internationally as well. ❖

Dr. Lydia Makrides, who directs Dalhousie University's School of Physiotherapy, is also the mover and shaker behind the $30 million Kuwait-Dalhousie Rehabilitation Project—the largest contract ever awarded to a university-based health care project in Canada. Photo by Jocelin d'Entremont.

Nova Scotia is the first community in the world to be served by a com-
prehensive TeleHealth Network—a sophisticated and yet highly practical
technology that links people in every corner of the province with specialized services in Halifax. Now this technology—developed in Halifax—is
being exported abroad. On the Caribbean island of St. Kitts-Nevis, for
example, people needing the advice of a radiologist can get an immediate and expert opinion within 24 hours. X-rays taken in St. Kitts-Nevis
are read by a specialist at the Halifax's Queen Elizabeth II Health
Sciences Centre, who sends back a report by the following day, via the
TeleHealth technology. Photo courtesy of TecKnowledge.

CHAPTER 6

FROM HERE TO ANYWHERE— HALIFAX'S GATEWAY ON THE WORLD

(Above) Captain "Bob" Power is a recently retired harbour pilot who has spent the past twenty five years bringing every kind of vessel through the entrance to the harbour. Photo by Jocelin d'Entremont.

(Left) Atlantic Container Lines, a Swedish-owned company, has its Canadian headquarters in Halifax. Sweden is Nova Scotia's largest foreign investor. Photo by Jocelin d'Entremont.

A Well-Traveled Crossroad

Halifax was created for trade and transport, a legacy which has shaped the city's history right from the beginning. Its most prominent feature—an extensive harbour gateway carved from bedrock by a glacier—was strategic to fishers and seafarers long before Halifax appeared on the map. Native Mi'kmaq people knew it as *Che-book-took*—"at the biggest harbour"—a sheltered summer encampment rich with forests, fish and wildlife. Early European visitors called it "Chebucto," a place where ships found safe anchorage as they journeyed to and from the fishing grounds on the Grand Banks. In 1749 the British built a permanent garrison on the site and called it "Halifax" in honor of Lord Halifax, who drew up the plans for its early settlement.

It is easy to see what attracts people to this spot, century after century. Halifax enjoys a location that is just as strategic now as it was on the day the city was founded. Fifty nautical miles from the shipping lanes of the Great Circle Route and significantly closer to Europe than any other port on the continent, the city is a natural crossroad. The British liked the harbour's secure anchorage and its accessibility—a short sail from the Saint Lawrence to the north, close to the French outposts at Annapolis Royal and Louisbourg, and a short trip by land or sea to the American colonies. They put Colonel Edward Cornwallis in charge of the new settlement.

Thirty-six years old and facing a challenging new assignment, Cornwallis's excitement on seeing Chebucto was evident. On June 22, 1749, within a day of his arrival, he wrote a five-page letter to his superiors back in London describing the land, the forests, the small pockets of French settlers, the abundance of fish . . . and the wonders of the harbour. "All the officers agree the harbour is the finest they have ever seen," he enthused.

Today, Cornwallis's assessment of the harbour still holds true. The strategic gateway that drew the visionaries of the past is more valuable than ever in a world bent on trade. With a seamless network of air, road, rail and sea links, Halifax is fast emerging as a competitive trade and commercial gateway to NAFTA, the Caribbean, Europe and the

---

Halifax enjoys a location that is just as strategic now as it was on the day the city was founded. Photo by Jocelin d'Entremont.

Mediterranean to the Suez and every corner of the globe. This is not new in a city where trading and seafaring are traditional, but the stakes are getting higher.

Captain "Bob" Power is a recently retired harbour pilot, who first saw the bridge of a ship from knee level while watching his father at work. He has spent the past twenty five years bringing every kind of vessel through the entrance to the harbour, threading his way between Chebucto Head and McNab's Island and on up to the container piers near the heart of the city. He can tell you exactly how many ships he has ushered in—more than eight thousand vessels from every corner of the world, each one recorded in neat handwriting in one of his pocket-sized bright red logbooks.

For Captain Power, guiding fellow seafarers is a blood tradition. There has been a pilot in every generation of his family since Halifax began licensing harbour pilots in 1829, and perhaps even earlier than that. Every contour of the passage is familiar to him, from the granite landmarks of the headland to the features of the ocean floor, and he describes them in the seaman's terms that count most in the shipping industry. "Ice-free," "sheltered" and "secure," with good anchorage that will hold a ship—these are clear advantages. Most important, the harbour's extraordinary glacial channel is sixty feet deep, and even deeper in the heart of the Bedford Basin—where convoys rallied during two world wars.

Halifax is easily accessible. From where the pilot clambers aboard off Chebucto Head to the modern container piers near the city's core is "about an hour's sail on a good ship" Captain Power will tell you. Other ports take half a day or more to bring a ship from the entrance to the dock—half a day of tugboat and pilot fees. It is an expense shipping companies can do without.

Halifax, 1750 A.D. Photo courtesy of Nova Scotia Archives.

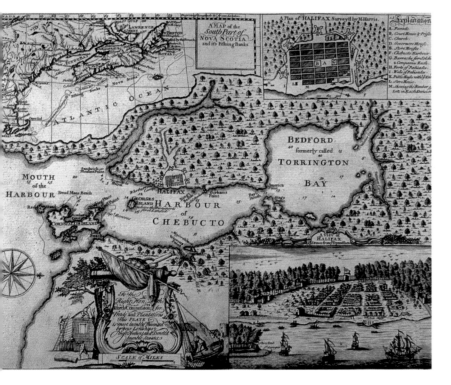

Tugboats are indispensable in the Halifax Harbour. Photo by Jocelin d'Entremont.

Smart gateway

Halifax's prime location and geological features come naturally. Generations of political leaders, admirals and traders have augmented these features with efficient infrastructure—particularly during wartime, when Halifax was a major naval base. Today, the port is more strategically important than ever. Halifax's modern shipping terminals are linked to an efficient rail network, transcontinental roads and Canada's fastest-growing international airport. The Port of Halifax is also becoming a "paperless" port. It has an electronic data interchange system that is the most advanced of its kind in Canada.

Competition between the Eastern seaboard ports is fierce, and huge amounts of capital are spent upgrading facilities and keeping channels clear. Halifax has a special edge that no amount of money can buy. The channel is naturally deep, and the city's geographic position gives it by far the shortest trip to Europe (and to Southeast Asia through the Suez Canal)—a full day's sailing shorter than any of its east coast competitors. Now the Halifax port and rail connection is also the fastest route between Central Canada, the US Midwest and overseas markets. The recently completed St. Clair Tunnel linking Sarnia, Ontario, with Port Huron, Michigan, has cut 24 hours off the Halifax-Chicago transit time. Canadian National Railways' new 75-acre intermodal terminal in Harvey, Illinois, means that more and more customers are taking advantage of Halifax's cost-saving double-stack train connections.

Halifax continues to be Canada's largest naval base, as well as home to the Bedford Institute of Oceanography, a world-renowned oceanographic and fisheries research institute. Today the harbour's naval and research vessels are being joined by growing numbers of offshore-related vessels as Halifax's oil and gas industry gathers momentum off the Nova Scotia coast. This project promises an abundant source of natural gas for homes and industries across Eastern Canada and the United States—and it adds yet another dimension to the Port's varied and complex

economy. Halifax companies like MM Industra and FABCO CKT have multi-million dollar contracts to provide infrastructure for offshore exploration and development. Secunda Marine is supplying support vessels for the project. Drilling platforms have begun appearing in the harbour, as has the Saipem S-7000—the largest "lift ship" in the world, with twenty-seven thousand tonne cranes on its stern. Lift ships are used to install prefabricated sections of the offshore drilling platforms.

If you could peek into the holds of the ships travelling up and down the harbour, you would find traces of every corner of the world. A whole gamut of products, widgets and creatures pass through here—cars, livestock, computer components and even entire houses. Several Nova Scotian companies are exporting prefabricated wooden homes to Germany. Acadian Seaplants produces carrageenan—a seaweed-derived food substance—and ships it to thirty or forty countries around the world.

Another company, Dover Flour, is so closely tied with the life of the Port, its offices have become part of the landscape—spliced in-between the grain elevator, the railroad tracks, the large, featureless sheds. Dover receives grain from western Canada and exports milled flour to places like Iceland, Bermuda and the Caribbean.

"Our business depends completely on the facilities here," says Dover President John Doering. "The Port is efficient, it is reliable, its rates are well-controlled and the location is ideal for trade . . . .

There are not too many places you cannot reach from here."

Halifax harbour's extraordinary glacial channel is sixty feet deep, and even deeper in the heart of the Bedford Basin-where these convoys were positioned during World War II. Photo courtesy of the Maritime Command Museum.

Highway to the future

In 1997 the Port of Halifax handled fourteen million metric tonnes of cargo—a figure that is increasing as new container lines keep arriving and as ships continue getting bigger.

That issue—the increasing size of container ships—is a make-or-break hurdle for most major ports, but it is working in Halifax's favor. Shipping experts are keenly aware that Halifax's deepwater channel puts the city in an ideal position to serve Post-Panamax vessels—ships too large to navigate the Panama Canal. There are not many other ports that can handle these deep-draft vessels without costly dredging.

As it is, the shipping trade relies upon Halifax as a "first port in, last port out" for vessels operating in the Atlantic trades. This not only ensures the fastest transit times, but also enables these large ships to discharge enough cargo to lighten them up for the next stop—where the water might be twenty feet shallower.

This is an auspicious sign. As the ships get larger and larger, they are also more expensive, which means they need to spend more time at sea and less time in port to be profitable. Therefore, more and more alliances of shipping companies are choosing to only call at a

few select "load centre" ports. And the experts agree that Halifax has what it takes to be successful in this new era of container shipping. Here's what the internationally renowned Moody's had to say in its recent *Port Ratings Outlook*, "Moody's expects Halifax to emerge as one of the container load centres on the east coast, based on the combination of a deep harbour, improved rail connections, an established market position, and a good carrier mix." Work has begun re-tooling the dockside facilities and new cranes are on order to handle Post-Panamax ships, which are significantly wider than conventional container ships. The transition demands enormous amounts of capital—there are some very large pieces of hardware involved—but that is simply today's challenge in a port with two hundred fifty bustling years of history.

Captain Bob Power does not have to climb rope ladders up the sides of heaving container ships anymore. "That's the part I do not miss—it is just too hard on the body," he admits, enjoying the comfort of his study. Still, he cannot stay away from the blowing sea spray, the rumble of engines, the comings and goings. The Captain works "on call" at the helm of tugboats two or three times a week. He is also an excellent draughtsman, rendering all kinds of ships in exquisite pen and ink detail—"some of them are actual ships, some of them imagined," he muses.

Whether you are sitting in a boardroom on the Halifax waterfront, operating machinery at one of the city's major terminals, or spending an afternoon the way Captain Power likes to do, cross-hatching the contours of a freighter with a fine quill pen, it is good to know that wherever your ideas may take you, you can easily get there from here. ⁑

For people who live on one side of the harbour and work on the other, the fun way to commute is on the Halifax ferry, which makes the crossing in just a few minutes. The views are great, the fare is cheap and you can unwind from work with a newspaper and some friendly conversation. Founded in 1752, it is the oldest continuous saltwater ferry in North America. Halifax resident John Conner ran the original service with a large rowboat. Photo by Jocelin d'Entremont.

The Port of Halifax is one of a minority of facilities around the world that track and record shipments instantaneously with electronic hand-held terminals. "Checkers" like Donald Miller of Halterm have said goodbye to their clipboards and are embracing a new way of doing things. Each time a truck approaches the gate, Miller records all the critical codes and the data goes straight to the computer. Photo by Jocelin d'Entremont.

TITANIC

"God himself could not sink this ship."

"Même Dieu ne pourrait pas couler ce paquebot."

It wasn't just the production crew that impressed me, but also the level of cooperation from government agencies, local vendors, equipment houses and hotels. Our shoot was pulled together in a very short period of time. If we hadn't received the kind of cooperation we did, I would have been in a very bad situation. It amazes me how we were able to cut through red tape and accomplish some of the things we did on *Titanic*. The Coast Guard, several branches of the military, even the office of Economic Development, bent over backwards to help us folks from Los Angeles—despite our daunting list of demands. And their efforts paid off. We were able to find the perfect studio site with our own private dock, close to the mouth of the harbour.

Halifax is a small city when compared to other film production centres. I was amazed at how much talent is packed into this compact area. It's a hotbed of creativity in a beautiful rugged environment. I wouldn't hesitate for a minute before going back to shoot there again. ❖

The Nova Scotia Museum's "Maritime Museum of the Atlantic" has a collection of *Titanic* artifacts and history that draws visitors from around the world—as many as 7,000 visitors in a single day during the busy summer season of 1998. This *Titanic* deck chair—on exhibit at the museum—was given to Halifax Reverend Henry W. Cunningham for his work performing services and burials for *Titanic* victims in the days following the disaster. Photo courtesy of Maritime Museum of the Atlantic.

At Halifax's Fairview, Mount Olivet and Baron de Hirsch cemeteries, 150 simple gravestones bear the same date—April 15, 1912. Halifax felt the impact of the tragedy in a way that affected people's daily lives for weeks. Photo by Jocelin d'Entremont.

CHAPTER 7

THE PEARL IN THE OYSTER—ARTS ALIVE

(Above) This circular Music Room (circa 1794) was built near the shore of Bedford Basin by Edward, fourth son of Britain's King George III, for his lover and companion, Therese Bernadine-Mongenet, better known as "Julie." Photo by Jocelin d'Entremont.

(Left) Maud Lewis (1903-1970) lived in this tiny house *(4.1m x 3.8m)* with her husband, Everett Lewis from 1938 until she died in 1970. Maud Lewis painted almost every surface in the house including everything from the door to the dust pans.

Halifax has a rich heritage and a vast array of cultural and entertainment facilities, including a repertory theatre, a dance company, a symphony orchestra, four movie sound stages, an entertainment arena that holds ten thousand people and an Imax theatre—to name but a few.

Shakespeare by the Sea's production of *Henry V*. Photo courtesy of Shakespeare by the Sea.

The concerts of the symphony orchestra—Symphony Nova Scotia—are broadcast live on national radio. The dance company is Gwen Noah Dance, a showcase for the work of a gifted Halifax performer and choreographer. The repertory theatre is the Neptune—with nearly 40 years of history and newly expanded stage and theatre school facilities.

Resources such as these—and there are many more of them—add layers to the city's lifestyle. You can watch a gritty interpretation of Shakespeare's *Henry V* in an open-air park, or hear the Symphony perform live at the Rebecca Cohn Theatre. And Halifax has creative energy that goes beyond a thrilling moment of performance. People come to the city from all over the world to pursue a creative agenda. They come to learn graphic design and visual arts at the Nova Scotia College of Art and Design (NSCAD) in the heart of downtown, or to study theatre, music or stage costume at Dalhousie University. They come because they have heard "the buzz" about the city's extraordinary film industry. Many of them come simply to be a part of one of Canada's most vibrant arts communities.

"Theatre people like to be here because of the vitality of this region," says Gay Silverman of the Nova Scotia Drama League.

Artist Eric Jensen is one of the 600 students attending the Nova Scotia College of Art and Design. Photo by Janet Kimber.

The Nova Scotia International Tattoo attracts big crowds as it celebrates the city's military history. Photo by Jocelin d'Entremont.

"The activity spans every level—from repertory to an annual Fringe Festival to the gutsy originality of the Alive Theatre group. A lot of original work comes out of here."

Originality, yes, but Halifax's arts community draws its strength from deep roots. A Halifax writer or musician is just as likely to challenge you with his or her "take" on traditional conventions as with a brand new idea. Drama, story-telling and music-making have warmed kitchens and community halls in this city for several generations. "We are very good at engaging people with stories that are real and distinctive—rarely bland," says Glenn Walton, a Halifax writer and filmmaker who teaches at the Atlantic Filmmakers' Co-operative.

The juxtaposition of tradition and invention is a fertile brew for creative minds. Halifax is attracting all kinds of artists—and a lot of young talent. "There's been a noticeable increase in the number of people who have been away and come back," says Rob Cohn, a Halifax culture entrepreneur who is best known as the founder of the East Coast Music Awards. "Kids want tall buildings, nightlife, streetlife, bars . . . they just want energy, and Halifax is blessed with a compact downtown area that has all that," says Cohn.

If there are gravitational forces at play here, the Nova Scotia College of Art and Design (NSCAD) is probably the biggest magnet. NSCAD is located in historic buildings downtown, right in the heart of the business district. It has 600 students in design, visual arts, film theory and art education, attracting students and professors from all over the world.

Andrew Terris heads up the Nova Scotia Cultural Network—an organization that represents the cultural sector and is working with the province to develop a strategy for future growth. Terris, a native of the Northeastern United States, came to Halifax in the 1980s and spent several years as a successful production craftsman before getting involved in the policy side of arts and culture.

"In terms of making this a lively, energetic city, I think NSCAD plays a really important role," he says. "It is the kids from the Art College who are starting bands and newspapers and cafes and film companies and computer animation companies. They are designing sets for films. They are influencing the way the city looks. That's what is giving Halifax its creative edge.

When I think of the number of young people who are working in the arts and culture industries here—it is just exploding!"

More than just a pretty picture

Arts and culture employs more than 21,000 people across the province—including some of the best and brightest Nova Scotia youth. The sector generates half a billion dollars' worth of direct revenues and an exciting range of opportunities.

Television co-productions with the Canadian Broadcasting Corporation alone are worth more than $30 million to the economy. That $30 million means more than cash in people's pockets. It means talent development for writers, producers and film crews. It means building Halifax's reputation as one of Canada's best television production centres—with front-running shows like *Street Cents, Theodore Tugboat* and *This Hour Has 22 Minutes*.

The success of Halifax's film industry reflects the quality of Nova Scotia writers, actors, set designers, visual artists, and much more. Filmmaking is a collaborative art, and the creative fabric here is rich with talent.

Music is another expression of Halifax's cultural vitality. Nova Scotia has 4 per cent of Canada's population and 14 per cent of the country's music royalties. The music industry is generating close to a hundred million dollars worth of direct revenues—on a par with the burgeoning film industry. Natalie MacMaster, Lennie Gallant and Laura Smith all recorded their first CDs in the state-of-the-art facilities at Halifax's CBC Radio studios. The Irish group *The Chieftains* recorded their most recent CD there—an album called *The Fire in the Kitchen.* They were drawn by the reputation of the Halifax production facilities and by the talent of local performers.

"There is a lot happening in music in Halifax," says Tanya Wolstenholme, the executive director of the Music Industry Association of Nova Scotia. The "*Johnny Favourite Swing Orchestr'* just signed an international deal with Universal—they are young musicians jumping in the swing music revival, and people love them. There is Marc Robillard, a 24 year old who started a record label called Drop Records—doing very well—and now he has two hot Halifax bands on his roster, '*Dr. Yellow Fever and The Jive'* and '*P.F. Station'*. They have recorded their first albums, and now they are touring through Ontario."

"These are just a couple of examples," says Wolstenholme. "We have a lot to be excited about."

Production crafts are also thriving. Buyers are coming from all

Gwen Noah, a gifted Halifax performer and choreographer, leads her own dance company, Gwen Noah Dance. Photo by Cylla Von Tiedemann.

The St. Thomas United Baptist Church Junior Choir in performance. Photo by Jocelin d'Entremont.

Andrew Terris heads the Nova Scotia Cultural Network, a non-profit agency that represents the cultural sector. Photo by Jocelin d'Entremont.

have broken into tough international markets by combining strong aesthetic values and savvy marketing. Now the arts community is working with business and the universities to develop a New Media Centre in the city—another partnership of artistic and entrepreneurial talent, lead by people who understand this is a winning combination.

"I'm really encouraged by the wide and thoughtful appreciation for the arts that is coming forward in this community," says Russ Kelley head of the Nova Scotia Arts Council (NSAC). NSAC is responsible for the provincial funding of professional artists and arts organizations, helping to maintain the high levels of excellence for which Nova Scotia artists are renowned.

"It's not just coming from a select community of arts-supporters. Government, corporations, universities—people from every quarter are actively providing financial, advisory and volunteer support to encourage and strengthen the wide range of cultural activities in this region. For a city the size of Halifax, the level of concern is quite remarkable, and it is one of the ingredients that is making Halifax a leading centre for arts and culture."

In today's climate of shifting technologies, there is pressure to acquire the knowledge and the tools that are critical to the future. This is merely the survival requirement—the background "scenery"—to a global drama that is transforming our lives, and our economy. If you are smart, creative and daring enough to design some of the "props"—perhaps even write part of the script—you can begin to dream a larger dream. With its blend of artistic and entrepreneurial talent, Halifax is poised to aim high and to achieve unprecedented wealth.

A smart, educated workforce, with the "creative capital" and independent-mindedness to build something brand new: properly tended, Halifax's artistic resources may well turn out to be the city's winning advantage—the pearl in the oyster. ❖

over Canada and the United States to invest in high quality Nova Scotia products. A company called "Spots Pots" is selling hand-painted ceramics throughout Canada and the United States. Two Halifax women—Lee Hopkins and Neal Doucet—are painting wildlife scenes on Nova Scotia slate and marketing them as far away as Japan. Tourists on the Halifax waterfront can watch master-craftsmen make hand-blown, hand-cut glassware at the Nova Scotian Crystal factory—Nova Scotian Crystal is the only workshop of its kind in North America. The hand-forged ironwork at "Urban Alchemy" is being marketed throughout the world through an innovative web site. There are all kinds of examples of local artists, writers and designers using the Internet to expand their client base to every corner of the world.

On its own, arts and culture is an outstanding asset to the people of this community, with no end in sight for its economic growth. But the bonus is the value arts and culture adds to all the other sectors, through "marriages" on key initiatives. That synergy was evident in the artistry with which Halifax hosted the G-7 Summit in 1995—with people like local artist Victor Syperek involved in designing sculptures, signage and streetscapes. Halifax film companies like Imagex and Salter Street

Symphony Nova Scotia. Photo by Jocelin d'Entremont.

Jeanette White is the director of the young Neptune Theatre Company and she also runs the Neptune Theatre School. "I tell the students, you are *artists*—you have the power to change the world." Neptune Theatre is one of Halifax's many live performance theatres and offers world class performances of a variety of plays and musicals. Neptune also offers theatre classes for children and adults. Photo by Ken Kam.

Halifax cartoonist Bruce MacKinnon at work. MacKinnon, an international award winner, is the cartoonist with the *Halifax Herald Ltd.* Photo by Jocelin d'Entremont.

The Soho Kitchen is a favourite haunt for Halifax's creative community. Owners Kyle Jackson, a former NSCAD student, and Tom Roussell have been cooking up soups, stir frys and mean desserts here for more than thirteen years—as well as collecting the whimsical Nova Scotia folk art that fills every nook and cranny. Photo by Jocelin d'Entremont.

CHAPTER
8

SMART CITY IN THE
NEW MILLENNIUM

(Above) Sacred Heart School of Halifax, a private girls' school, is
one of Halifax's many private schools. Sacred Heart School of
Halifax opened its doors for the first time in 1849.
Photo by Jocelin d'Entremont.

(Left) Halifax celebrates a rich history and looks forward to a bright
future as it stands on the threshold of a new millennium.
Photo by Jocelin d'Entremont.

Dale Godsoe is a Halifax native who has been actively involved in community affairs throughout her life—with a particular interest in contemporary media and education. She serves on the board of a number of prominent organizations, including MTT, Viacom Canada Limited, the Women's Television Network Foundation and the Canadian Centre for Philanthropy and is a past president of the YWCA of Canada. Godsoe is Vice-President External at Dalhousie University.

I would say, in the last ten years, the change that has been most evident to me has been a renewed optimism about our future. I see it here, at the university, in the way people are embracing challenges. They are saying—"alright, we can do this much—but if we do it in partnership with someone else, we can add another layer of expertise. And if we add an outreach to another continent or another part of the country, we can bring that much more value to the program, and to the students, and to the research going on here in Halifax."

John Brannan is the President of Sable Offshore Energy Incorporated—a Halifax-based management consortium of Mobil Oil Canada Properties Ltd., Shell Canada Ltd., Imperial Oil Resources Ltd., Nova Scotia Resources Ltd. and Mosbacher Ltd. SOEI is directing a $3 billion project that will bring ashore 3.5 trillion cubic feet of natural gas, and distribute it by pipeline to markets in Nova Scotia, New Brunswick and New England—with first gas planned for the first of the new century.

The Sable Gas project is already having a major impact on the local economy. If you add up all the people that are working on this project right now, it's easily over 2,000, and this thing is going to keep getting *bigger*. Not only that, for all the jobs directly created by Sable there will be four or five times that in indirect jobs. So if you are not working on the project you are working for somebody else that is working on the project, or you are selling groceries to someone who is working on the project. Employment is the highest it's been in Nova Scotia in a long time. Tourism is up. All the restaurants, the hotel occupancies are up. I don't think there is any doubt that Sable is part of that picture. The Royal Bank, the Toronto Dominion and others that publish reports have said that our economy is growing and Sable is having an impact. And this project is just a very small piece. There is 18.5 trillion cubic feet of reserve out there. Our project addresses about three and a half trillion cubic feet.

The world is watching this project. We will deliver our part of Sable gas on time, and on budget. That sends out a strong message.

(Right) McNab's Island occupies the mouth of Halifax Harbour. Historically, McNab's Island was part of Halifax's defense system. Today, the island offers visitors natural beauty as well as history. Photo by Jocelin d'Entremont.

(Below) John Brannan, President and General Manager of Sable Offshore Energy Incorporated. Photo by Jocelin d'Entremont.

Outstanding community volunteer, Dale Godsoe is Vice President External at Dalhousie University. Photo by Jocelin d'Entremont.

Lori Covert is a marketing analyst who runs a full service advertising agency, Vantage Communications. Photo by Jocelin d'Entremont.

Fred Smithers, President of Secunda Marine. Photo by Jocelin d'Entremont.

It's a matter of achieving long term viability through short-term credibility. Halifax is going to come out a big winner!

Lori Covert is a marketing analyst who lives in Halifax and runs a full service advertising agency—Vantage Communications. Covert's career has had some landmarks that reflect her strong forward-looking instincts. Together with her business partner and husband, Michael, Covert invested in the first on-line video-editing suite in Canada. Now their company is expanding as a result of their growing expertise in the oil and gas industry—a highly specialized area. One of Vantage Communications' largest clients is Sable Offshore Energy Incorporated.

I am in love with this place. Lifestyle is a big component of that, obviously, but I am a pretty business-minded person. For me this is a place where you get the best of both worlds.

There are real advantages to working out of Halifax, and one of the biggest is the time zone. We can do business with clients in Europe and the West Coast of Canada in the course of a single day. You know how people talk about the "global economy"—well it's here, and we are in the right place. I travel a lot. I can get everywhere from here. And from an IT perspective, I have access to people with a very high standard of training. McKenzie College and the Nova Scotia Community College are turning out people with exceptional multimedia skills.

Working with "Sable," it is hard not to get excited about how big this is. I think that without a doubt the Sable gas project is going to be the most significant economic event to hit this province. Even at this early stage it is putting a lot of money into people's pockets. When you think of the amount of gas resource that is out there and the interest being shown by international oil and gas companies, it is really phenomenal.

In Aberdeen, with North Sea oil, originally they had to import a lot of expertise. But gradually there was a transfer of knowledge. Now they are at a point where they export knowledge. That is what is happening here. On a small scale it is happening in my company, because here we are working for Sable, and oil and gas companies

are coming to us from all over the world. They perceive that through our involvement in Sable gas, we are getting a real handle on the offshore industry—and that is true.

I have to be honest with you—I did not foresee that this would happen. I was excited to have Sable as a client, but I did not understand how big it was going to be. I feel that Halifax is at a very pivotal point in its growth and development. It is going like crazy, and it is nice to get in on the ground floor.

Hector Jacques is a native of Goa who came to Halifax in the 60s to study engineering at the Technical University of Nova Scotia. He has lived here ever since. Jacques is the Chairman and CEO of Jacques Whitford—a geoscience and environmental engineering consulting firm with 640 employees and $75 million worth of annual revenues. Jacques Whitford has its corporate headquarters in Halifax, as well as offices across Canada and in New England and joint ventures in Buenos Aire, and Trinidad.

I did a project for a Canadian client in Argentina, and the report was sent back and forth between here and Buenos Aires three times. Do you realize the telecommunications cost of sending a seventy-page report between here and Buenos Aires three times was little more than a Tim Horton's coffee and donut? You could not do this ten years ago. Jacques Whitford is a worldwide domain. You can send anything to anybody in this company, at "Jacques Whitford dot com," it does not matter whether that employee is in Buenos Aires, Russia or right here in Halifax. We are a "virtual office." On one project we have going right now we have people from six different cities working together, not all of them in the same country.

I think the future for Halifax looks great. The key is good government. Right now we are growing, we have one of the lowest unemployment rates in Canada. As long as our taxation rates are competitive with other parts of North America, as long as our business climate continues to move in a positive way, then we will be able to attract talented knowledge workers and retain them. That is what counts in the knowledge economy.

Fred Mattocks, Regional Director of Television for the Canadian Broadcasting Corporation. Photo by Jocelin d'Entremont.

Fred Smithers is a marine owner-operator who heads a company called Secunda Marine. He bought his first ship with a couple of partners in 1983—the Tartan Sea. *Now he has eighteen ships working in waters around the world—from service and supply ships for offshore drilling platforms to cargo vessels, three salvage tugs and a high-tech cable laying ship. Secunda Marine has been contracted to supply the service vessels for the Sable Offshore Energy project.*

Oil and gas development is going to be one of the best things that ever happened to this province. It is bringing all new money into the region—and that money is starting to circulate. I see it with our own company. We've got four vessels on with Mobil Oil right now—that's a huge contract, it really is. There are probably 150-175 men working on those vessels—Nova Scotians making big money. We have had to increase our operations here, hire staff. We have two trailers loaded with people, until we put the new addition on. Talk to anybody in the real estate business now. There are a lot of people moving in because of Sable Gas. And it is not just high-end people who are benefiting. The people who work for me are regular Nova Scotians. We have a lot of fishermen who work for us, about six hundred employees. I can see where this phase of the Sable Island gas development won't be complete, and the next project will be started—there's no doubt in my mind. We've worked in West Africa, in the North Sea, in Ireland . . . everywhere we've worked it's happened the same way.

Fred Mattocks is the Regional Director of Television for the Canadian Broadcasting Corporation (CBC) in Halifax. The CBC has played a key role in building the growth and the high standards of Halifax's film and television industry—investing in co-productions like This Hour Has 22 Minutes, Black Harbour, Theodore Tugboat *and* Pit Pony, *and broadcasting them across the network. The CBC is an important vehicle for talent development locally and nationally.*

I am very excited about what I am seeing in this community—not only in the film and television industry, where I work, but across the board. It almost feels like there is a "critical mass" of things happening. Everywhere you go in Halifax, there is a film crew working, there is a television series in progress, there are actors moving around. There are people like Ken MacIntosh, at the Royal Bank, who looks after the film industry. He's up to his ears in film production. A banker involved in film production! Bill McGilvray's *One Heart Broken Into Song* just finished wrapping. Chris Zimmer is involved in a bunch of projects. Andrew Cochran is putting together twenty-six half hour episodes of *Pit Pony*. Salter Street is burgeoning at the seams. We've got organizations like the Centre for Art Tapes and the Atlantic Filmmakers Cooperative which are developing new talent and finding new ways to turn their money into programs and new possibilities. There's a whole new awareness of this industry as a really rich R & D environment that fits very well with the positioning of Halifax as a "Smart City" full of knowledge workers. Film and television is a knowledge industry.

The synergies we are seeing develop between the cultural community and the wider community are absolutely fundamental to our future. We have groups like TARA (Telecom Applications Research Alliance), Innovacorp, we have key players in the government . . . if all these people come to the table with the same broad goals and the same willingness to contribute what they can to a larger success, the momentum will just keep growing.

Denis Ryan became well known across Canada as a member of the popular Irish singing trio, "Ryan's Fancy." Today, Ryan is still an active musician and performer—but he has also become a prominent figure in the Halifax business community. In 1996 Ryan brought master craftsmen over from his native Ireland and opened "Nova Scotian Crystal" on the city's waterfront—Canada's first hand-cut, mouth-blown crystal factory.

That was a dream I had—bringing over the craftsmen and starting a factory in Halifax, passing on the skills to local youth. I was always fascinated by the craftsmanship of that particular industry—the intense fire, the blowing and the cutting. . . I remember the day we started up the furnaces for the first time—it was like a symphony, seeing it all fired up.

My ambition is to see Nova Scotian Crystal become a brand name

Denis Ryan, owner of Novia Scotia Crystal, Canada's first hand-cut, mouth-blown crystal factory. Photo by Jocelin d'Entremont.

(Above) Bernie Smith, Nova Scotia's Deputy Minister of Finance. Photo by Jocelin d'Entremont.

(Left) The Public Gardens were established in 1867, the year of Confederation. They were opened to the public in1875. Photo by Jocelin d'Entremont.

and Design (NSCAD)—some of us feel quite strongly that NSCAD is a wonderful resource. If you look at the things that have grown—like the film industry—that's an obvious example of how NSCAD supports economic development. There are all sorts of examples across the province—people who are working successfully as a result of their training at NSCAD. NSCAD and our universities are being seen as engines of economic growth—as they should be.

I think at the moment, for the first time in 125 years, this province is on the verge of booming. Nova Scotia was a very wealthy part of Canada before Confederation disrupted all the natural trading patterns. Now, with NAFTA and the EEC, trade patterns are realigning in our favor—North—South. The knowledge revolution works in our favor as well. Our level of Internet usage is one of the highest in Canada. People are marketing their expertise all over the world, from here in Halifax. Not just in things like engineering and communications—it is happening in the Arts community as well. People are exporting their music, their fabric designs, using the Internet.

Suddenly, it seems as though the things we have here are *right* for this particular time. The planets are lining up.

The best part is that this is a very caring society too—a city with a heart. I've often thought it would be an interesting way to compare cities if you had a measurement of their "dropping times"—how long it takes people to offer assistance if someone collapses on the street. I can think of several cities where it could be days. In Halifax everyone would be rushing to pick them up before they hit the ground!

There is a sense of fun about this place and a willingness to take chances too. I've been here thirty years now and I can't imagine living anywhere else. ❖

in Canada, in North America, maybe around the world. We are starting up a mail-order business now. I would like to see it grow to a point where we are hiring 200 skilled workers. We have 25 people working there at the moment—masters and apprentices. We have a great president and CEO, Rod McCulloch. We have only been in business two years and it has already grown a lot. I believe we can build a global business here and create some opportunities for our young people at the same time. In this business, training young people is the future—that's how the knowledge is passed along.

Bernie Smith is Nova Scotia's Deputy Minister of Finance—a position he assumed recently after an interesting and varied career in both the private sector and municipal government. He was in charge of Finance for the City of Halifax—now amalgamated into the Halifax Regional Municipality. He has been active in a number of areas that are important to Halifax's economy, including the pharmaceutical industry and the film industry. Prior to becoming Deputy Minister, Smith played a key role in establishing "Electropolis"—a movie sound stage on the Halifax waterfront.

Is our economy growing? You bet it is! We are going to be first or second in Canada this year in terms of growth—and it is not just because of the development of our oil and gas resources offshore. Our pharmaceutical industry is growing. This province is ideally suited to become a major test bed for pharmaceutical products. I think the music industry will take off as well. The IT community is doing important work. We have a renewed interest in artistic activity, a booming film industry. Modern communications. The whole economy is moving—you can see that.

One of the things, of course, is the arts community is making a tremendous contribution. We have the Nova Scotia College of Art

As a seafaring community for 250 years, Halifax will be celebrating the new millennium with a spectacular Parade of Sail! The city of seven official ports of call for the Tall Ships 2000 race, which will cross the Atlantic—from Genoa, Cadiz and Southampton to Bermuda, Boston and Halifax and then finishing in Amsterdam. The Tall Ships will be in Halifax during the month of July-year 2000. Photo by Jocelin d'Entremont.

PART II

LEADERSHIP

9

BEDFORD INSTITUTE OF
OCEANOGRAPHY, 84-87

HALIFAX REGIONAL WATER
COMMISSION, 88-89

NOVA SCOTIA LIQUOR
COMMISSION, 90-91

MARITIME FORCES ATLANTIC, 92-93

MTT, 94-95

Photos by Jocelin d'Entremont.

BEDFORD INSTITUTE OF OCEANOGRAPHY

Mysterious, dangerous, vast, and powerful—the oceans are a major component of our planet's ecosystem.

Exploring A Vast Resource

Salt water covers nearly three-quarters of the earth's surface and affects our weather, the seafood we eat, even the air we breathe. Understanding how changes in the ocean affect human life and, conversely, how man's activities affect the ocean is vital to long-term sustainability of life as we know it. Research is the answer to understanding the ocean. Scientists at the Bedford Institute of Oceanography study the ocean—how and why it changes, how it moves and how its physical, chemical, biological and geological processes work, individually and together. Though not as vast as space, the deepest depths of the oceans might just as well be on Mars. The challenge to reach those depths and understand animals and a land mass we can't see drives scientists to devise ways to explore this unknown frontier that surrounds us.

In and under the ocean, enormous quantities of natural resources swim in the water column or lie buried in the bedrock— fish, shellfish and marine plant stocks; oil, natural gas and minerals which can mean economic sustainability for generations of Canadians. With one-third of Canada's Gross National Product (GNP) generated by activities that, in one way or another, use the coastline directly or as a transportation route, Canada must collect information about all aspects of its ocean resource. This information is vital for land-use planning and in reducing risk from natural hazards. As well, our coastline provides important habitats to hundreds of species of birds and wildlife.

Scientists cooperate with fishermen to better understand, conserve and manage fisheries' resources.

The Facility

The Bedford Institute of Oceanography (BIO), which opened in 1962, is located on the shores of Halifax Harbour and is Canada's largest centre for ocean research.

The first major federal centre devoted to oceanography, the Bedford Institute has grown to rank among the most respected ocean research institutions in the world. Its scientists and research facilities are a major source of inspiration and support for companies and institutions which need ocean knowledge in their business.

BIO is administered by the federal department of Fisheries and Oceans in cooperation with Public Works and Government Services Canada, both on its own behalf and for the other departments that maintain laboratories and researchers at the Institute.

The Institute's 40-acre campus comprises a complex of buildings with 36,000 square metres of floor space, of which 12,000 square metres are devoted to scientific laboratories. Scientists at BIO perform targeted research mandated by government, such as advise on marine environments (including fisheries and hydrocarbon resources), production of nautical charts from Georges Bank to the Canadian Arctic, and responses to environmental emergencies.

Together, about 350 scientists, engineers and technicians contribute to the research undertaken at the Bedford Institute. Supported by research vessel crews, maintenance personnel, computer programmers and administrative and library staff, the Institute provides employment for approximately 600 people in the Greater Halifax region.

The Canadian Coast Guard operates the Science vessel fleet and supports

The Bedford Institute of Oceanography

Beach development and stability studies are an important part of GSC Atlantic marine research program.

specific research projects from its other vessels, specially in the Arctic Ocean.

The Institute's oceanographers are fascinated by the ocean and want to understand it. They study it constantly—ever patient, observant of minuscule changes and working as a global team with other scientists to piece together the puzzle that covers most of our planet.

The Partners

The partners housed at the Bedford Institute are Fisheries and Oceans (DFO) Canada, Natural Resources Canada (NRCan), the Department of National Defence (DND), Environment Canada (EC), Public Works and Government Services Canada (PWGSC) and Health Canada (HC).

Fisheries and Oceans Canada is represented at the Bedford Institute by six divisions of its Science Sector, including the Canadian Hydrographic Service (CHS). Together, they provide scientific knowledge and advice on a wide variety of issues related to climate, oceans, the environment, and marine fish, mammals, shellfish and plants.

DFO's scientific team delivers a constant flow of new knowledge from its ongoing research programs to solve present problems and to take advantage of current and future opportunities.

Since the passage of Canada's Oceans Act in 1997, DFO has focused attention on ocean management. This has meant increased awareness of, and involvement in, activities such as community education and capacity building, development of tools for integrated coastal and marine management (e.g. resource mapping), and facilitation of broad stakeholder participation in ocean management initiatives. New concepts such as Integrated Management, Marine Protected Areas and Marine Environmental Quality Standards require much scientific input, as well as new research, to further the knowledge required for sound decision making and management.

Natural Resources Canada is represented at the Bedford Institute by the Geological Survey of Canada (Atlantic). It is the country's principal marine geoscience facility, and its scientific research expertise is recognized worldwide.

GSC Atlantic's team of over 100 specialists focuses on marine

and petroleum geology, geophysics, geochemistry, and geotechnology. The centre is a source of integrated knowledge and advice on Canada's coastal and offshore land mass. As such, GSC Atlantic provides information to a wide variety of clients, including consultants, resource industries, government agencies, educational groups and the general public.

A diverse, internationally recognized research program of geological, geochemical, geophysical, and geotechnical studies is undertaken at GSC Atlantic. These studies, organized into three components, provide expert information on the coastal zone, the seabed and offshore sedimentary basins, as well as the related processes, and contribute to assessments of resources, hazards and environmental quality.

Canada needs more information about all aspects of its geology and land mass. Applications of GSC Atlantic's geoscience knowledge and technology transform raw material into value-added products, key to economic growth in natural resource industries.

GSC Atlantic scientists also try to increase the well-being of Canadians by identifying and attempting to predict natural hazards in the environment, such as earthquake zones. Internationally, GSC Atlantic will continue to participate in science ventures that indicate a clear net benefit to Canada in terms of cost-shared research or potential market opportunities for Canadian industry.

The Department of National Defense supports its ocean surveil-

Electronic charts and tridimensional bathymetry help improve marine safety.

lance activities through the Maritime Forces Atlantic's Route Survey Office. In cooperation with CHS and GSC Atlantic, surveys of areas of the sea floor of specific interest to DND are conducted.

The Seabird Research Unit of Environment Canada (EC) conducts seabird and pollution analysis, studies migration habits and monitors breeding colonies for long-term effects of pollution and the depletion of principal food sources. EC's Environmental Protection Unit analysis water samples for pollution control and for legal purposes when prosecutions take place under federal anti-pollution laws.

A Collaborative Approach

DFO at the Bedford Institute of Oceanography serves its clients in close cooperation with DFO's Gulf Fisheries Center located in Moncton, New Brunswick, and St. Andrews Biological station located at St. Andrews, New Brunswick. Both DFO and NRCan work closely with universities, private companies and other government agencies and participate in many international projects.

Responding to a Public Mandate

Some of BIO's current priorities, established by the public agenda, include the state of fisheries resources, sea level rise, offshore development, coastal zone management, climate changes and territorial claims. BIO experts are relied upon to deliver their knowledge and advice to the federal government on these issues as they are affected by the oceans.

Many of the Institute's projects are interdisciplinary, bringing together physical, chemical, biological and geological oceanographers, who strive to find the answers to age-old questions about the sea.

Some projects are international, involving scientists from other oceanographic institutes around the world working side by side for the common good and a global understanding of the oceans.

The shaded relief map of a multibeam bathymetric survey of Halifax Harbour provided vital information to a client determining the location of a sewage treatment plant.

Scientific teams at BIO investigate the physical and chemical properties of the ocean, the life within it, and the geology of the sea floor, as well as the interactions between the atmosphere, the oceans and the continents. In fact, many of the scientific studies undertaken at BIO trace the influence of the oceans on the health and well-being of human life itself.

At any one time, teams of BIO scientists are involved in more than 150 oceanography

The study of the tectonic evolution of the North Atlantic and Arctic Oceans provides insights into the development of sedimentary basins for establishing resource potential.

projects. Specific fields of application include Ocean Science, Climate Studies, Fisheries Research, Marine Environmental Geoscience, Marine Chemistry, Habitat Ecology, Ocean Mapping and Seabird Research and Management.

Scientists at the Bedford Institute work closely together to carry out their research activities. They also share information with the private sector and other departments. Using and developing state-of-the-art technologies, they study all aspects of the ocean from the atmosphere above it to the bedrock beneath it. Some of the current activities undertaken by the Bedford Institute and its collaborators include:

• Fisheries research monitors stock status for many exploited species, studies life cycles and population biology, multi-species interactions within ecosystems, and the impact of fishing efforts on future population trends.

• Biological Oceanography seeks understanding of the structure and function of marine ecosystems, including the role of the marine microbiota in the planetary carbon cycle, and how they can be studied using imagery collected from satellites.

• Habitat Ecology studies the human impact on aquatic environments and endeavors to save or restore marine habitats.

• Physical Oceanography seeks to understand, describe and eventually predict changes in the physical environment of the oceans,

nated Canada's Strategic Centre of Excellence for Towed Array Design and operates the largest towed array manufacturing facility in Canada. Its products are in use by the Canadian Navy and work is currently underway on the next generation of fully distributed digital telemetry arrays for use on Canada's City Class Frigates.

The Future

The advent of new technologies has dramatically shaped the approach to maritime surveillance, and the Halifax region has responded aggressively. Businesses are working together to link capabilities to meet current and future requirements. Hermes will remain as a local leader and looks forward to enhancing its reputation for innovation and technical achievement within the community.

On a worldwide basis, what has always set Hermes apart has been its unmatched commitment to customer support and service. From its emphasis on ISO 9001 and Total Quality Management philosophies, to its use of advanced Material Resources Planning, Hermes continues to build on its half-century of success to push the edge of the technological envelope. The continuing consolidation taking place in the defence and aerospace industry is viewed as an opportunity for Hermes and Ultra to expand both their technology base and market breadth.

Hermes values its reputation for innovative and technical achievement. Building strong relationships with customers worldwide has been, and will continue to be, vital to Hermes' growth. "Competitive prices, proven technology and innovative solutions result in market growth and customer loyalty," says Mr. Trowse. "Outside our traditional Canadian and U.S. markets, we've grown from base sales of 5 per cent in 1992 to nearly 50 per cent in 1997."

Looking to the future is an everyday occurrence at Hermes Electronics, a company with its foot already in the 21st century. ⁕

CBC TELEVISION–HALIFAX

Bustling with energy and ideas, CBC Television in Halifax is a hotbed of creativity, employing all types of people who transcend the traditional image of government employee. Their interest in and passion for all facets of community life here on the east coast is tangible and visible through CBC Halifax's unique programs and productions.

The physical headquarters of CBC Television's Halifax station leaves conflicting impressions—of a modest 1950s style building—and a state-of-the-art television production facility that produces award-winning programs. Inside this four storey building and smattering of auxiliary trailers, there's an array of talent and technology that tells the real story of CBC Television's Halifax operation.

Maritime People, Maritime Flair

Vision, energy, creativity, cost-effective partnerships, business savvy and state-of-the-art production facilities—these are the hallmarks of CBC Television. However, it is the people working at CBC Television who are the unique component behind its success. Halifax's 250 years of heritage offers a tremendous foundation for programming that portrays the distinct personality of the Maritimes and its people. Fred Mattocks, Regional Director of Television for the Maritime Provinces says, "Almost all of the people who work here are from the Maritimes. The others live here by choice. They *are* CBC Television and they are deeply rooted in this community."

CBC Television's Halifax station received the International Gabriel "Station of the Year" award in 1997. Competing against television stations across North America, CBC Television in Halifax won for its programming commitment to the community. Mattocks notes, "It isn't one person or program that won this prestigious

award—it is the collective efforts of a diverse group of people. We transform a variety of talents and ideas into programming that reflects who we are. The excitement that permeates CBC Television in Halifax is well known and envied across the country."

Partners in Programming

CBC Radio One and CBC Radio Two, also located in Halifax, are creative partners with CBC Television, particularly on the East Coast music scene. This successful relationship is evident in joint productions that have received national and international accolades.

Nova Scotia's former education minister, Hon. Robbie Harrison, speaking at the 1998 East Coast Music Awards, likened the energy

it alone. And the partnership works both ways—groups and organizations come to us with ideas; other times we look specifically for corporate partners, arts organizations or individual artists who have a story to tell and need a venue and/or production assistance. In this way, we uncover ideas that reflect the people and the experience of living in the Maritimes."

A Canadian Perspective

CBC Television's Halifax station is also home to CBC Newsworld, Canada's 24-hour network that provides more hours of original live programming, live news specials and live in-depth news analysis than any other service in Canada. Every morning, Newsworld is broadcast live from Halifax, exploring the impact of world events on Canadians.

Success Breeds Success

Over its 40 year history, CBC Halifax's program successes have included among others, the nationally televised political satire, *This Hour Has 22 Minutes*, the internationally successful *Theodore Tugboat*, multi award-winning *Street Cents*, North America's only youth advocacy consumer show, as well as some of CBC Television's most popular and long-running shows, including *Don Messer's Jubilee*.

CBC Television gives a Canadian view of the world. At CBC Halifax, that view is distinctly Maritime in flavour—just the way people like it. ✛

and talent for music and cultural excellence in the Maritimes to an "onshore energy" which may rival offshore development as an economic base for this region. According to Mattocks, "CBC Television is well aware of this potential."

CBC Television in Halifax is a viable, living, growing force to be reckoned with. As a business entity, it is efficient and resourceful, and like other organizations in the 1990s, doing more with less. Its programming reflects the stories, voices and characters of this region, working closely with other groups and organizations within the community, such as Salter Street Films, Brookes Diamond Productions and others who showcase the culture of the Maritimes.

CBC is very proud of its links to the community through this broad range of creative partnerships. Mattocks says, "We could not do

SABLE OFFSHORE ENERGY INC.

Saipem 7000, heavy lift crane, in Halifax Harbour. Halifax Citadel is in the foreground.

More than three decades have passed since Mobil Oil Canada and Shell Canada first acquired permits to explore for oil and gas off Nova Scotia's shores. Discoveries in the 1980s were not exploited due to high development costs, low oil prices and the lack of immediate markets. Today, however, the Sable Offshore Energy Project has moved from the exploration phase, which merely explored potential, to development, with tangible benefits for the citizens of Nova Scotia and for Canada. Although Nova Scotia has been an oil producer since the early 1990s, the Sable project marks the province's debut as a gas producer.

The Sable Offshore Energy Project involves producing natural gas from one of the largest known natural gas deposits left to be developed in North America. The six fields under development are Venture, South Venture, Thebaud, North Triumph, Glenelg and Alma. The $2-billion first phase of the Sable project will see the development and production of natural gas from three of these offshore natural gas fields (Thebaud, Venture and North Triumph) on the Scotian Shelf near Sable Island.

Shareholders in the project's operating company, Sable Offshore Energy Inc. (SOE Inc.) are Mobil Oil Canada Properties Limited, Shell Canada Limited, Imperial Oil Resources Limited, Nova Scotia Resources Limited and Mosbacher Operating Limited. SOE Inc. received sanction in Halifax in February, 1998. As well, the province of Nova Scotia, its residents, suppliers and contractors are deeply entwined in this project.

Exploration Continues

Sable is designed to recover in excess of 3.5 trillion cubic feet of proven natural gas reserves. In fact, the Geological Survey of Canada predicts that the Scotian Shelf probably contains at least a further 13 trillion cubic feet of natural gas.

Exploration companies have already started the search for these hidden reservoirs. In 1998 alone, oil companies bid a record $562 million for the right to explore blocks of undersea real estate in the offshore regions around Nova Scotia. These new developments will keep Nova Scotia and Halifax's economies growing for many years to come.

Leading the Economy into the 21st Century

Nova Scotia is on the threshold of a new era of economic growth. The Sable project forms the foundation for a vibrant new industry in this part of Canada. Nova Scotians are already feeling the effects of having an average of one million dollars a day pumped into the economy, and SOE Inc. is expected to generate $80 million a year in payroll and taxes alone.

The benefits of the oil and gas industry are many. Obviously it generates employment and economic prosperity through royalties and taxes. But, as demand for goods and services grows, the industry attracts many other businesses to invest in the local economy. Communities grow with infrastructure to service the offshore industry. This will mean future generations of Nova Scotians will have more career opportunities in their home province.

Santa Fe Galaxy II Jackup Rig.

Load out of de-ethanizer for transport to Goldboro Gas Plant Site.

The Process

Offshore and onshore facilities will develop, produce, transmit and process the expected 500 million cubic feet of natural gas per day. Gas and the associated natural gas liquids from the offshore production platforms will be brought ashore by a 225-km subsea pipeline to the processing plant at Goldboro, Guysborough County.

The natural gas liquids will then be taken by onshore pipeline northeast to a fractionation plant at Point Tupper, Cape Breton. The sales gas will be transported to Nova Scotia, New Brunswick and New England markets through a separate 525-km Maritimes and Northeast Pipeline project which will tie Nova Scotia and New Brunswick into the existing North American gas pipeline grid in the

Fabrication of Thebaud & Venture Jackets at MM Industra yard, Dartmouth, Nova Scotia.

northeastern states. Pipeline construction will contribute about $750 million in direct spending to the province, and the multiplier effect due to "indirect" jobs is anticipated to be four times that amount.

The Prospects

The economies of other coastal areas of the world where natural gas and oil have been discovered, such as Aberdeen and the Gulf of Mexico, have grown strong and vibrant from oil and gas production. Oil drawn from the North Sea over a quarter of a century ago led to Aberdeen's development as Europe's "Oil Capital," employing more than 40,000 people in the oil and gas industry—and its status as one of Europe's more prosperous cities.

Metropolitan Halifax, as the project head-quarters, will also enjoy tangible benefits of the Sable project and the growing oil and gas industry infrastructure. Manufacturers, consultants, contractors and service companies in Metro Halifax, throughout Nova Scotia and other parts of Canada will have new opportunities to compete in supplying goods and services as the industry grows. As well, education, training, research and development associated with the project will maximize the employment of Nova Scotians.

Another benefit to Nova Scotia will be the investment in local communities. Canadian petroleum companies and their employees take their corporate and individual responsibility very seriously, making positive contributions to all facets of the communities in which they operate. In recognition of Sable Offshore Energy Inc.'s commitment to the Nova Scotia community, The Society of Fund Raising Executives named the organization "Outstanding Corporate Philanthropist" in April 1999.

Future Prosperity

As the Sable Offshore Energy Project construction proceeds, millions of dollars are being spent in this area. The Atlantic Provinces Economic Council (APEC) counts 30 new energy projects in the region worth an estimated $30 billion over the next eight years. As industry knowledge and technology improves, new opportunities to use the infrastructure that is being created for Sable will emerge. The current development project and subsequent ones will sustain Nova Scotia's economy for decades to come. ❖

TRANSPORTATION, MANUFACTURING & DISTRIBUTION

11

Photos by Jocelin d'Entremont.

HALIFAX PORT AUTHORITY

Mervyn Russell, Chairman of the Board, Halifax Port Authority.

"All the officers agree, the harbour is the finest they have ever seen!"
—Captain Edward Cornwallis, 1749

The Port of Halifax is much more than a deepwater ice-free port. Founded in 1749, the Port is a source of pride, a place steeped in history, an industry that has resulted in billions of dollars in economic activity in our region and country—a key vehicle for economic development.

Halifax Port Authority was established in 1999 by The Honourable David Collenette, Minister of Transport, pursuant to the Canada Marine Act. The Halifax Port Authority is the federal agency (succeeding the Halifax Port Corporation) responsible for managing and marketing the Port as a thriving productive resource and sustainable asset for the benefit of the local, regional and national economies. It creates an environment and industry conducive to the successful operation of the Port and its users.

Halifax's Greatest Natural Resource

Halifax is the deepest container port on the North American East Coast, offering a natural harbour depth in the main shipping channel of over 18 metres (60 feet). It is a port of call for over 20 direct liner services that operate on all major trade lanes; and coastal feeder vessels servicing ports in Newfoundland, New England, and the French islands of St. Pierre and Miquelon.

Located on the Great Circle route, the Port offers the shortest ocean voyage between North America and Europe, and for ships operating on Round-the-World and Suez routings. A full day's sailing time can be saved by using Halifax as first inbound or last outbound port of call, enabling shipments to reach their destination faster than via other East Coast gateways.

Success in the shipping industry depends upon timely and cost-effective port calls. The Port of Halifax offers some of the lowest container costs and quickest ship turnaround times of any major North American East Coast port. And thanks to the Port's advanced Electronic Data Interchange system, customs clearance and documentation are effected smoothly, well before the goods reach their destination, for additional savings in time and money.

Most port facilities at Halifax have direct, on-dock rail service as part of Canadian National's (CN) North American-wide network. Double-stack trains move daily from the docks in Halifax to markets in Central Canada and the U.S. Midwest. CN's investment in its St. Clair Tunnel, which runs under the St. Clair River, between Sarnia, Ontario, and Port Huron, Michigan, creates opportunities for Halifax to penetrate new markets in the United States. Since its opening in 1994, container traffic to the U.S. Midwest, moving over the Port of Halifax, has increased almost fivefold.

In 1998, the Port of Halifax handled 13.2 million metric tonnes of cargo, including 3.5 million metric tonnes or 425,000 TEUs (twenty-foot equivalent units) of containerized cargo.

As a primary Canadian conduit for international trade, the economic impact of the Port of Halifax is significant and far-reaching. Approximately 7,750 direct and indirect jobs and $520 million in employment income province-wide are generated through activities relating to the Port of Halifax.

Port Facilities

Most businesses achieve their success by having a new talent or by developing and investing in opportunities. The Halifax Port Authority continues to build on the Port's historic strengths and profitable record as a dynamic, world-class port of call while seeking new prospects. Stakeholders at the Port have earned a reputation for commitment and productivity that is vital to the Port's success.

David Bellefontaine, President and Chief Executive Officer, Halifax Port Authority.

The Halifax Port Authority is responsible for regulating and administrating operations within Halifax Harbour defined as "all waters lying northeast of a line running north 56 degrees east and distant 1,066m Southeasterly from Pleasant Point, and including the waters of Bedford Basin and the Northwest Arm."

Container Terminals

Halifax International Container Terminal, operated by Halterm Limited, is located at the entrance to Halifax Harbour limits. Opened in 1969 as Canada's first common-user container terminal, it operates four berths with depths of up to 15.1 metres (50 feet). The 72-acre facility is equipped with four ship-to-shore gantry cranes with support equipment for on-shore container handling, two roll on/roll off (ro/ro) ramps and 245 in-ground outlets for the safe storage of refrigerated cargo. Halterm Limited's customers include some of the world's largest international shipping lines. Its recent order of two post-Panamax cranes, to be delivered in 2000, will equip the Terminal to handle the latest generation of post-Panamax container vessels.

Fairview Cove Container Terminal, operated by Cerescorp Company, offers 660 metres (2,165 feet) of continuous berth space serviced by three 40 tonne ship gantry cranes with support equipment. The 69-acre facility, located at the north end of Halifax Harbour, includes a ro/ro ramp, 250 reefer outlets and on-site storage for over 9,000 TEUs. Doubling its capacity since opening in 1982, this Terminal has further expansion capability on land and water. It too counts the world's leading container operators among its clientele.

Both terminals deliver 24-hour service, seven days a week, and are equipped to handle container, break-bulk, heavy-lift and ro/ro cargo. Daily CN double-stack train departures ensure third morning delivery from dockside into Chicago. Commodities handled at the two facilities include forest products, mechanical and electrical machinery, chemicals, peat moss, metal and perishables.

Breakbulk Terminals

Ocean Terminals, the traditional heart of breakbulk activity at the Port since 1917, offers 13 deepwater berths for a diversity of cargoes such as forest products, steel, rubber, flour, heavy-lifts and offshore supplies. Over 37,945 square metres (408,000 square feet) of covered storage is available with direct loading to ship, rail or truck.

Pier A, Ocean Terminals was re-engineered in 1997-98 creating an additional deepwater berth, a specialized forest products facility and additional laydown area for containerized and project cargo operations. The Canadian Society for Civil Engineering designated Ocean Terminals a National Historic Civil Engineering Site in 1998.

Richmond Terminals is a multi-purpose common-user facility centrally located for highway and rail connections. The Halifax Port Authority recently re-engineered Pier 9A into an efficient terminal for combined breakbulk, container and heavy-lift operations. Richmond Terminals also serves as a supply base for offshore drilling activity.

The Port of Halifax bustles year-round, boasting an ice-free harbour with natural depths of 18 metres (60 feet) with tidal variations of 1.5 metres (5 feet) or less.

The inner harbour at the Port of Halifax is approximately 16.7 kilometres (9 nautical miles) long and 2.8 kilometres (1.5 nautical miles) wide.

The Port is well equipped for heavy-lifts and project cargo like this ro/ro shipment of a 138.75 metric tonne tunnel boring machine.

Grain Elevator

The Port of Halifax plays a key role in the logistics chain, handling the majority of import and export cargo for the grain elevator. Wheat received by Halifax Grain Elevator is destined for export markets, milled into flour by Dover Mills Limited or utilized by the agricultural industry as domestic feed. As an alternative to rail, transportation by water has lowered shipment costs by as much as $20 per metric tonne for the domestic feed industry.

The Halifax Grain Elevator facility has a maximum loading capacity of 2,000 metric tonnes per hour, and a marine leg maximum unloading capacity of 700 metric tonnes per hour. The self-unloader unloads at a rate of 1,200 metric tonnes per hour. Maximum storage capacity of the elevator for wheat is 140,000 metric tonnes; slightly less for corn or barley.

Breakbulk cargo comes in many forms, like this shipment of paper products. Together with specialized equipment and skilled stevedoring services the Port can handle it all.

Cruise Industry

Halifax is a full-service cruise port within easy walking distance to downtown. It is one of the most popular ports of call on the New Atlantic Frontier, that includes seaports in Atlantic Canada, the St. Lawrence, the Northeastern United States and St. Pierre and Miquelon.

The Seawall, at Ocean Terminals, is the Port's principle cruise facility measuring 612 metres (2,007 feet) encompassing Piers 20, 21 and 22. In 1999 Halifax Port Authority opened its Cruise Pavilion at Pier 21 as part of its continuing commitment to the cruise sector. Over 200,000 cruise ship passengers and crew will transit Halifax Port Authority facilities in 1999 with direct spending by passengers exceeding $7.0 million.

Pier 21, a National Historic Site, is the last immigration shed in Canada. Between 1928 and 1971, over a million immigrants, refugees, war brides and children began their lives in Canada at Pier 21. It was also the embarkation point for 500,000 Canadian troops during World War II. The Pier 21 Society Immigration Exhibition Centre, located on the upper floor of the Halifax Port Authority Cruise Pavilion, commemorates and enlightens residents and visitors alike to this historic role of the Port.

Privately Owned Facilities

The Halifax Port Authority is responsible for creating an environment where private operators can compete successfully and serve clients efficiently.

Dover Mills Limited, a tenant of the Port Authority, began producing flour in Halifax in 1968. Connected by pipeline to Halifax Grain Elevator for maximum efficiency, Dover Mills, the largest Canadian-owned mill, is capable of producing 270 metric tonnes of flour each day. In 1997, Dover Mills Limited became the first flour mill in North America to achieve ISO 9002 accreditation.

Most of Dover's flour is milled from Canadian Western Red Spring wheat. In addition to serving Atlantic Canada and Quebec, Dover Mills exports to the United Kingdom, France, the Caribbean, Bermuda, Iceland, West Africa and Japan. Dover Mills Limited supplies numerous

Grain is discharged from the loading spouts into the hold of a ship at a rate of 2,000 metric tonnes per hour.

third-world nations through the Canadian Government's Food Aid Programs.

Each year, nearly 100,000 vehicles travel through Autoport, one of North America's largest vehicle processing and transshipment facilities. Operated by Autoport Limited, it received ISO 9002 certification in 1997, becoming the first vehicle processing and transshipment facility in North America to receive this designation. Specially designed to handle high volume ro/ro traffic of passenger vehicles, commercial trucks and tractors, Autoport's 100-acre facility is complete with secured storage and direct loading to truck and rail.

National Gypsum Wharf, owned and operated by National Gypsum (Canada) Ltd., provides an interface for raw gypsum delivery from rail to ship. By specialized railcars, raw gypsum is delivered to the port facility, located on the shoreline of Bedford Basin, where it is loaded by conveyor into ships' holds. National Gypsum (Canada) Ltd. operates the largest open pit gypsum mine in the world, located in Milford Station, just outside of Halifax. Over three million metric tonnes of gypsum are exported over this facility each year, for use primarily in construction trades.

Imperial Oil Limited is both a customer and a service provider at the Port of Halifax where it operates a refinery, three wharves and a bunker fuel service. Coastal and foreign-going tanker vessels are loaded and discharged at Imperial Oil's wharves which are connected to its refinery by pipeline. A crude oil receptacle conveys the imported raw product from larger foreign-trading ships' holds to the on-shore refinery. Exported refined fuels, lubricants and home heating oil are processed, then conveyed back through the system to smaller coastal tankers for distribution to markets in Canada and the United States.

Imperial Oil Limited's bunker operation provides fuel and lubricants to the marine trade using the Port of Halifax. Its bunker barge, the Imperial Dartmouth, can be seen plying the waters of the inner harbour with its cargo of 1,700 metric tonnes of intermediate fuel and 500 metric tonnes of marine diesel oil. Ship bunkering can be accommodated at any location within the harbour, either at anchor or dockside by barge.

The Port of Tomorrow

The Halifax Port Authority is working with customers and stakeholders to ensure competitiveness as a modern and progressive port of call.

The Authority's approach to the future is based on the combination of profitable growth and responsible investment with the goal of ensuring private sector operators have a world-calibre facility, that is both cost-effective and efficient.

The industry trends toward strategic carrier alliances and the deployment of larger, post-Panamax ships have significant implications for ports. Halifax is the only container port in Eastern or Central Canada capable of handling these huge vessels and offers real strategic advantages in terms of voyage transit times and vessel turnaround. By leveraging the Port's natural attributes with coordinated investments by stakeholders, Halifax Port Authority is optimistic about the Port's future in this new era of shipping.

Together in partnership with those who work at the Port, private sector operators and the community, Halifax Port Authority is working to ensure that Halifax's heritage of 250 years of profiting by the sea will continue well into the next millennium. ❖

The Port of Halifax has achieved international acclaim as a safe, popular and growing port of call, welcoming 15 cruise lines in 1999.

HOYT'S MOVING AND STORAGE LTD.

Their professional expertise, combined with their enthusiasm, assures a successful future for Hoyt's.

The moving business has changed over the years—there are now third-party companies involved who decide which mover handles corporate moves. These decision makers are located all across Canada, and Hoyt's makes the investment of time and money in getting to know and understand their needs.

Hoyt's understands what relocating families are going through, and has the expertise to make the process simple, efficient and professional. Trained moving consultants, supported by the entire network of companies affiliated with Hoyt's, move clients to national and international destinations with ease and assurance. Randy Hoyt, Director of

Leonard Hoyt the Mover began doing business in Halifax in 1940. Founded on the principles of respect and quality service for all customers, the company is still family owned and operated. Today the Hoyt's Moving and Storage Ltd. is recognized as the largest moving, storage and electronics distribution company in Atlantic Canada and dominates the specialized transportation market.

Having earned a sterling reputation in a very short time, Leonard Hoyt the Mover quickly became a well-known enterprise in Halifax. In 1949, he incorporated to become Hoyt's Moving and Storage Ltd. Expanding into the national market in the 1950s, Hoyt's became the first moving company in Canada to relocate a customer from coast to coast by highway van.

Following Leonard's death in 1961, the reins fell to his eldest son, Clifford. Under Clifford Hoyt's leadership, Hoyt's expanded from a one-city Halifax moving company to an Atlantic Canada-wide organization, by establishing branch offices throughout Nova Scotia, New Brunswick and Newfoundland.

Hoyt's was one of the founding members who, in 1953, established United Van Lines Canada Limited as a Canadian member-owned van line. Clifford Hoyt, a former president of United, claims two advantages from this affiliation—room for personal attention to local business while benefiting from nationwide vehicle coordination, advertising and purchasing.

Clifford Hoyt is very proud to have his three sons, a daughter and a younger brother now working for Hoyt's Group of Companies. They form an integral part of the dynamic team that leads the company today.

One can't help but get caught up in the enthusiasm expressed by this younger generation. Like their father and grandfather before them, each takes pride in having learned the business from the ground up.

Sales and Marketing, notes, "The company is very resourceful at finding solutions. A worry-free move is what Hoyt's clients expect, and they have come to trust that that's what we'll deliver."

Planning and attention to every detail make every move a success at Hoyt's. With its own history of expansion and relocation, Hoyt's understands that the success of any office move is measured by the sustained productivity of staff while the move is planned and executed. Efficiency cannot be compromised, and the move must be completed with minimal interruption. Moving consultants work closely with clients to plan the entire process according to the client's schedule. Site supervisors at origin and destination ensure that every piece of furniture and equipment ends up correctly installed in the right location. Hoyt's warehouse management system (WMS) keeps track of each item, as well as billing and inventory.

While their business is still traditionally 80 percent long-distance and local residential and commercial moving, the remaining 20 percent of Hoyt's clients require "specialty services"—moving high-tech electronics equipment and other delicate commodities. The Specialty Service Division of Hoyt's Group, started in the early 1990s, handles relocation, distribution, configuration and warehousing of electronics throughout the region. The Specialty Services Division also moves and installs automated banking machines for all of Canada's major banks. Gentle handling of sensitive equipment is guaranteed, and Hoyt's factory-trained technicians have the expertise to assemble and install machinery.

These "high-tech" and "high-value" commodities cannot be transported like just another carton or crate. Hoyt's success in this area is based on its investment in sophisticated tracking and security systems, as well as competent, well-trained employees, to assure the client's peace of mind.

Hoyt's commitment to Atlantic Canada has led it to invest in real estate, building new warehouses and offices, and the hiring of local staff in each of the many Atlantic Canadian communities where Hoyt's operates. The company's involvement in the region, however, goes way beyond the services it offers to customers. Hoyt's has been a long-time supporter of minor league sports, and managers and employees are encouraged to participate in service clubs and other community activities.

Hoyt's management team acknowledges that the experience gained as truck drivers and other jobs in their early years with the company has taught them to value the people who built Hoyt's with their hard work and reliability.

Randy Hoyt sums it up this way: "The dedication and commitment of our employees, many of whom have been with us for more than 25 years, is key to our success. Like the Hoyt family descendants of Leonard Hoyt who have made Hoyt's their career, many other employee families have second- and third-generation family members working here. They enter a client's home or office and inspire trust that the job will be well done. To each of them we say, 'well done'." ❖

THE OLAND BREWERY

Endurance in the Face of Change

Since 1867, the Oland Brewery has stood for pride of craftsmanship. First brewed in the family's Dartmouth home, Susannah Oland's "October Brown Ale" was the beginning of a brewing tradition that continues to provide the people and communities of the Maritimes with beers of unrivaled quality. Generations of Olands have brewed beer with an enduring sense of common heritage, dedicated to traditional Maritime values for a true Maritime taste. Passed from son to son, this brewing tradition has been a source of pride that has allowed the Oland family business to prosper through the most challenging times.

From the devastating fires of the Halifax explosion to the dry years of Prohibition and through two World Wars, the Oland family remained committed to brewing fine beers. A legacy of endurance and strength in the face of adversity has kept the family dream alive and made the Oland name synonymous with extraordinary beer.

The Oland family of fine beers, including Schooner, Oland Export and Oland Premium Red, has also become synonymous with Halifax and the Maritimes. And no beer is more symbolic of Nova Scotia, in particular, than Alexander Keith's India Pale Ale. When the grand-daughter of this renowned brewmaster and former mayor of Halifax finally decided to sell the family business in 1928, she chose a brewery with the same dedication to brewing quality beer as the Honourable Alexander Keith himself. The Oland Brewery has since made Keith's a household name both in the Maritimes and in many homes across Canada, where their favourite beer represents a little of Nova Scotia in every bottle. The true taste of the Maritimes, Keith's is recognized by the Taste of Nova Scotia Quality Brands food program.

Pride of Ownership

The Oland Brewery also maintains a unique relationship with its employees. The union executive is directly involved in decision-making, ensuring the voice of all employees is heard. Oland Brewery's innovative approach to union-management relations has been a model for breweries internationally. "Our employees share our sense of pride and our vision to brew the best," says Oland's President Michael Glover. "Ownership promotes commitment; and commitment promotes personal best, which is the secret of our success as a brewery. 'Our brewery, our best, our future' is our employee slogan, evidence of the employees' belief in the company. We're very proud of our ability to work toward a common goal."

Leadership, responsibility, and commitment to excellence are standard at the Oland Brewery. Hailed by environmental groups as the ultimate example of responsible packaging stewardship, Oland has been reusing and recycling its packaging and raw materials for 75 years, decades ahead of other industries. The company, like other breweries across Canada, has invested millions of dollars to create a refillable infrastructure and the most cost-effective environment within which to facilitate return and reuse. Embraced by consumers, who return nearly 100 per cent of refillable beer bottles year after year, the deposit-return system incorporates the three R's of waste management: Reducing the manufacture of new bottles by reusing each bottle until it is recycled to make new glass.

The Oland Brewery's reputation as a brewer of great beers has withstood the test of time and attracted brewers of other fine beers seeking a place in the Maritime market. In the early 1970s, Labatt Breweries of Canada forged a partnership with the Oland Brewery based on Oland's success, knowledge of the market and expertise in brewing quality beer. Under this partnership, the Oland Brewery is responsible for brewing Labatt Blue and Budweiser, the most popular beers in Canada and the United States respectively. Oland brews Budweiser for the people of the Maritimes, under license from Anheuser-Busch. As well, the Oland Specialty Beer Company, created by Labatt in 1997 to market a diverse portfolio of leading international beers, chose Alexander Keith's India Pale Ale as its flagship brand, bringing the Oland Brewery's fine tradition to all Canadians.

More recently, Labatt Breweries of Canada became the newest member of the Interbrew family, one of the world's most successful

The Oland Brewery has been a Halifax landmark since 1867.

benefiting the entire region and spreading Maritime hospitality around the world. As well, ongoing investment in Oland's Halifax operation contributes $50 million directly and indirectly to the local economy each year. The company's brewing and recycling facilities provide stable employment for a large workforce.

Also symbolic of Oland's commitment to the Maritime community is its restoration of Alexander Keith's Original Brewery building and the establishment of a working, period-style brewing and operations museum in the city of Halifax. The project, targeted for completion in the year 2000, will bring new life to the south end of Hollis Street and help to enhance the Halifax waterfront. Says employee Peter Oland, founder Susannah's great-great-great grandson, "This initiative will have a positive effect on tourism and will make people aware that we've been doing what we do for a very long time. Visitors will leave with a greater appreciation of the history behind one of North America's oldest brewing traditions."

brewers with more than 400 years of dedication to the art and science of brewing. The relationship between Interbrew, Labatt and the Oland Brewery establishes a brewing heritage with some eight centuries of combined tradition and brewing excellence. Here in Canada, the Oland Brewery represents one of the most accomplished members of the Interbrew family.

While the Oland Brewery is undoubtedly the most visible promoter of beer in Nova Scotia, it has also proven to be a leader in promoting the responsible use of its products. "We're proud that Maritimers make our beer a part of their good times," says Oland. "But we view our ability to make and market our products as a privilege rather than a right, so we're continually looking for new ways to present the message of moderation to our consumers."

"We have a significant investment in Halifax and in the entire region," continues Oland. "Our history is their history and our legacy is their legacy. We're recognized as true Maritimers; honest, genuine and hardworking, wherever we sell our remarkable beers." ❖

True Maritime Taste

The Maritime community has made the Oland Brewery the successful company that it is today. And at Oland, giving back to that community goes well beyond sponsorships and affiliations. The company's support of community initiatives is far reaching, encompassing sports, arts, entertainment and charities. Events such as the Labatt 24-Hour Relay, the Halifax International Busker Festival and the Halifax International Tattoo have helped to put Halifax and Nova Scotia on the tourist map,

SWEDWOOD CANADA LTD.

Swedish furniture giant IKEA is well known for its huge and popular selection of inexpensive, modern furniture, most of which is manufactured in modules for home assembly. A huge player in the contemporary furnishings marketplace, IKEA's supply of North American furnishings is made in Greater Halifax by a workforce of 150 woodworkers at Swedwood Canada.

Swedwood Canada was founded in Sweden by Swedwood AB in 1986. At that time, the company had an agreement with IKEA to supply its North American products. Swedwood Canada was purchased by IKEA in 1991, and since then, IKEA North America has been the firm's only customer.

Located in Burnside Industrial Park, on the shore of Halifax harbour, Swedwood Canada processes particle board into flat furniture assembly kits for distribution throughout IKEA's North American retail outlets. The plant's 150 employees produce and distribute Billy bookshelves, Kurs dressers and other IKEA top-selling furniture items to the chain's stores across Canada and the United States.

Preparing its North American market launch during the mid-1970s, IKEA chose Halifax as the site of its first superstore. Halifax was chosen partly because it is the closest ice-free port to Europe, with an efficient shipping network between Europe and North America. Tommy Holmer, plant manager, adds, "The business environment in Nova Scotia was a positive one, and the welcome we received from Halifax and the province of Nova Scotia was very encouraging."

Holmer says that nearly 75 per cent of Swedwood's products go to the United States, making Swedwood Canada a major export company in the Greater Halifax area. The company ships up to 2,500 products a day and has aggressive plans to double that figure in the near future. Swedwood also imports some of the raw materials needed to complete the manufacturing process, including special fittings from Europe, through the Port of Halifax. Some veneer (a new technique that will be part of the company's future growth) is also shipped from Europe. As well, the company relies on truck and rail services to deliver to markets in Montreal, New Jersey and Los Angeles.

Swedwood Canada buys its particle board mainly in the Maritimes and elsewhere in Canada, while the firm's day-to-day requirements are easily met within the large Burnside business park. The company's growth has been impressive—having doubled its production capacity since 1991. Holmer says Swedwood will continue to expand during the coming three years.

Swedwood Canada has also made tremendous investments in its employees. Production workers have received extensive training to turn the raw materials into furniture items. Holmer adds that Swedwood is reaping the benefits of this investment. "We are fortunate to have many skilled employees who have been with us since the beginning."

Several years back, Swedwood Canada faced a decision about whether to grow the business in Halifax or move its production facility closer to American markets. Holmer notes that the decision to stay in Greater Halifax was due in part to the highly motivated and well-trained workforce and the similarities of Nova Scotia to Sweden. He adds, "The positive business climate and the support from government and the local business community solidified our decision to stay in Halifax." ❖

BUSINESS & FINANCE

12

Photos by Jocelin d'Entremont.

GREATER HALIFAX PARTNERSHIP

The Greater Halifax Partnership is a private enterprise registered in the Province of Nova Scotia, whose mandate is to promote growth and investment in the community. The Partnership is unique in Canada, and it has become a national model of cooperation between the private and public sectors.

The local Halifax business community deserves strong praise for the Partnership's success to date. Their significant financial investment clearly demonstrates a commitment to taking an active role in shaping the future of this region.

The Partnership itself grew out of opportunities offered by the 1996 amalgamation of four communities into the Halifax Regional Municipality. The response to the Partnership's establishment by the Halifax corporate community has been impressive. In 1999, more than 90 private companies have invested in the Partnership's operations. This private funding represents nearly sixty percent of the Partnership's annual budget. The largest public investor in the

Partnership is the Halifax Regional Municipality for which the Partnership carries out exclusive marketing, promotion and investment attraction activities.

The Greater Halifax Partnership's priorities are straightforward:
- Look after business in our community
- Grow business in our community
- Bring new business to our community

Eighty percent of the Partnership's energies are focused within the community. "Look After Business in our Community and Grow Business in our Community." Building investment in people and building confidence within the community are essential for prosperity. Site Selectors claim that in the next decade, eighty percent of all the new jobs created will come from companies already present in our community. As a result the Greater Halifax Partnership has mounted an extensive local awareness campaign, to build confidence and optimism within the community. Central to this campaign is branding Halifax *Canada's Smart City*.

Halifax is a newly restructured city, with a growing information technology community, five universities, two community colleges, a number of private training institutions, the largest student population per capita in North America, and a new oil and gas industry.

But, in 1749 when Halifax was founded, it was the harbour that attracted European settlement, and the city quickly became a major trading center. Today Halifax is still a key Canadian centre for trade and commerce. The region is ideally situated to take advantage of communications with the rest of the world during the 24-hour business day. Halifax conducts business in Europe and other eastern points in the morning, the mid-continent during the day, and California and western points late in the workday. By air, Halifax is less than two hours from New York, Boston or Toronto, and less than six hours from London, Stockholm or San Francisco.

By sea, the Port of Halifax is a full day closer to Europe than the Ports of New York, Baltimore or Montreal, with multi-modal transportation routes to all major North American regions. As well, the Port of Halifax is the only North Atlantic Port capable

The Greater Halifax Partnership Team. Back row, left to right: Melissa Oliver, Michael MacDonald, Paulette Payne, Stephen Dempsey. Front row, left to right: Bryan Burns, Nancy Phillips, Ruth Cunningham.

"Smart City Smart Move" is the trademark for Halifax, Nova Scotia.

of handling Post-Panamax ships. Halifax's coastal location is finally coming into its own at the end of the century. Post-Panamax ships, fast ships and trans-shipment, together with private investment in the port and airport, are all part of the new mix that makes Halifax Canada's Atlantic Gateway.

History, size and location then have made Halifax an international trade center. The Partnership has focused on three external markets: Sweden, the Atlantic Seaboard and the Caribbean Basin. In responding to the needs of the existing business community, the Partnership created the Canadian Swedish Business Association (CSBA) in 1996. Sweden is the largest foreign investor in the Province of Nova Scotia. The CSBA is a vehicle to join people and businesses together, and to develop investment between Greater Halifax and Sweden.

Within the Caribbean Basin the Partnership is working with Halifax universities and their Caribbean-based alumni. Before Confederation, Nova Scotia was one of the largest trading centres in the world, and much of our trade was with countries in the Caribbean Basin and Mexico. By expanding our trade opportunities with these regions, and within NAFTA, we are going 'back to our future'.

Business alliances and partnerships are essential to doing business in a global economy. December of 1998 saw the Partnership form a strategic alliance with Washington, DC, through the Greater Washington Initiative. This alliance gives our business community easier access to a community of more than 2,300 high-tech companies employing more than 260,000 people - a region second only to California's Silicon Valley. There are tremendous opportunities for Halifax-based companies to build their business in Greater Washington, and the Partnership is leading an aggressive campaign into this region.

The Partnership also actively recruits new businesses to the community. With the best-educated workforce in Canada, and the most universities per capita in North America, Halifax is a major player in the new, knowledge-based economy. A KPMG study has identified Halifax among the top five places to do

business within North America, Europe and Japan and the number one place to do business in the Life Sciences. A Globe and Mail study places Halifax in the top three cities in Canada in which to live and work.

In 1999, Halifax has had a high rate of business expansion and has been successful in attracting a large number of national and international companies. New corporate citizens include companies such as Arrow Electronics, Keane Canada Inc., Cisco Systems, Convergys Marketing, ITC Learning, Silicon Graphics, Mobil Oil, Shell, and PanCanadian Resources. Today's knowledge-based economy depends on brainpower for growth - and in growth Greater Halifax leads the country. Smart City Smart Move. ✦

Mike Cowie, a local entertainer, performs during one of the Greater Halifax Partnership's promotional events. *Halifax: Positively Magnetic!*

HALIFAX

ROYAL BANK FINANCIAL GROUP

Royal Bank Financial Group's Atlantic district head office in downtown Halifax.

Royal Bank Financial Group (RBFG) traces its roots back to the Merchants' Bank of Halifax, established in 1864. Now, as then, Halifax is the economic and geographic hub of the Atlantic region and remains a strategic location for RBFG. As the new century begins, RBFG is Canada's leading financial services institution and proud of its continuing connection with the city of Halifax.

Today's banking customer is changing—and so is Royal Bank Financial Group.

Banking customers today, whether retail, commercial, business or personal, are sophisticated, knowledgeable and value-conscious. Each customer brings unique needs, requiring creative, customized approaches to ensure that his or her financial goals are met. Working as an integrated team, member companies of Royal Bank Financial Group continue to adapt in a rapidly changing industry. Many Royal bankers, for example, are now trained in securities and mutual fund management and offer personal financial planning advice and counsel.

Royal Bank Financial Group believes that the effective delivery of quality financial services and advice is based on developing solid long-term relationships with clients, each with different financial goals and expectations. Throughout the communities that make up Greater Halifax, RBFG offers its personal and business banking clients a full range of banking, trust and investment products and services, delivered through a network of 21 branches, its Halifax Business Banking

Centre, International Trade Centre, Royal Trust and RBC Dominion Securities offices.

A Family of Companies

RBC Dominion Security Companies is Canada's foremost full-service investment dealer. As such, RBC Dominion Securities' hallmark is its ability to offer clients a broad range of investment choices and services, backed by the professional opinions of investment advisors and research analysts. The firm is a Canadian leader in adopting a disciplined, long-term approach to portfolio management techniques.

By custom-tailoring investment recommendations to suit each client's circumstances, RBC Dominion Services investment advisors help clients create and maintain lifelong, personalized investment strategies. Advisors work with clients to plan estates, manage existing wealth and prepare for retirement. RBC Dominion Securities' investment in technology, combined with its extensive list of research publications, economic reports and product information, means clients have everything they need to make informed investment decisions.

Royal Bank Action Direct

For those clients with a firm grounding in the fundamentals of investing, Royal Bank Action Direct discount brokerage offers a wide range of services to help them manage their investment portfolios. With Action Direct, clients save money—up to 88 per cent over full-service brokerage commissions—on equity trades while maintaining full control of their investments. Clients can place stock orders; trade mutual funds, GICs, and fixed income investments; obtain stock and options quotes; and transfer funds to and from their accounts by either telephone or computer.

Royal Bank Financial Group believes that the effective delivery of quality financial services and advice is based on developing solid long-term relationships with clients. Clay Coveyduck is Royal Bank's Senior Vice-President & General Manager for Atlantic Canada.

Royal Trust

Royal Trust is a carriage-trade name, dating back to 1899. Its business revolves around the management, custody and transfer of wealth for both personal and institutional clients in Canada and around the world. Royal Trust's expertise in the areas of personal and institutional trust services, mutual funds, investment management and securities custody services greatly enhances the strengths of Royal Bank Financial Group.

Both clients and industry have long regarded Royal Trust as a market leader and the only Canadian trust company with

120

MARKETPLACE

14

Photos by Jocelin d'Entremont.

COURTESY CHRYSLER

Before beginning his automobile career, Allan Dwyer, president of Courtesy Chrysler, was a schoolteacher with a desire to teach children and a strong belief in family. Though far from the classroom, these elements of his personality are clearly evident today at his award-winning Chrysler dealership. One of Canada's most successful dealerships, Courtesy Chrysler has outpaced the competition while retaining its "family-run" feeling. Greeted at the reception desk by Dwyer's wife, Judy, customers receive a personal welcome and unsurpassed attention to detail.

The mission statement posted throughout Courtesy Chrysler includes these words: "Demand excellent service, quality products and competitive value."

The words of customer Peter Arnburg of Dartmouth, Nova Scotia, offer proof that the company has succeeded in its mission.

In a letter to Allan Dwyer he wrote, "We needed a dealer who would respect our intelligence, provide an extensive choice of vehicles and superior service. Courtesy met all of these, getting our business because of the professional, caring reputation." Dwyer is building his customer base one car owner at a time, giving people a feeling of "membership," along with a sense of trust and belonging, even family.

That caring reputation is due to Dwyer's unique and subtle approach to marketing. While the superior Chrysler product sells itself, Dwyer promotes his dealership and his team through image building. In 1998, Courtesy Chrysler received the much-coveted Canadian Auto World "Marketer of the Year" award for a successful promotion that involved a Canadian tradition, CFL (football), and family values (children). Desired by dealers all over Canada, this award

is definitely not won by following the crowd. The "Accelerator" award goes to the one person or dealership that has demonstrated proven success in going faster and farther in automotive marketing, sales or promotions.

Chrysler Canada declared Courtesy Chrysler's Grey Cup promotion an outstanding example of innovative marketing that boosts both dealership traffic and community goodwill. The judges noted that Courtesy benefited from a concept true for business and life in general—"follow your interest"—in this case that meant kids and football.

Dwyer has done extremely well for a car salesman who got off to a late start. Just 12 years ago, in fact, he was selling cars for the competition, even earning the title of top salesman in Atlantic Canada for a local Nissan dealership. In late 1989, Dwyer felt the urge to be more independent, to operate his own dealership. He and his wife, Judy, whom he acknowledges as his right arm, sold their home and began their quest for the right combination of facilities and employees. In late 1992, the Dwyers, along with two business partners whom he has since bought out, purchased a Chrysler dealership on Dartmouth's busy Windmill Road. For someone who has been a senior manager for such a short period, Dwyer has learned quickly. He acknowledges there were growing pains throughout and is confident he has now achieved the "right team" to provide the best level of service to his customers.

In 1995, the company built a new facility at 461 Windmill Road. The new dealership boasts a spacious and bright, cheery showroom, clean, modern service bays, a larger lot and Metro's only Chrysler drive-through service area. Business has proportionally increased, Dwyer says, fulfilling his belief that customers like dealing with a modern facility offering convenient services. "It makes them want to come back."

Since 1992, Courtesy Chrysler's sales and service team has doubled in size, from 35 to 70. Dwyer is quick to acknowledge his good people skills and knack for picking the right people for the job. He has one of the best General Sales Managers in Canada, John Ryerson, and he claims his staff in the body, service and parts departments know more about cars than he'll ever learn.

"I have an excellent group of people around me, and it's very motivating," Dwyer explains. Angus H. MacLean, Lower Sackville, Nova Scotia, agrees with Dwyer. He wrote, "I would like to commend Mr. Allan Dwyer, president of Courtesy Chrysler, for having such competent and courteous staff involved in the repair and service of my vehicle. As long as I can rely on the kind of customer service supplied by Courtesy

Chrysler, I will continue to drive a Chrysler product."

Dwyer takes very seriously his role as employer—safety consultants have been used extensively to ensure employees are safe on the job. He explains, "There can be no compromise on safety in our workplace, nor in the job we do on our customers' vehicles. Our philosophy is not to sell cars but to provide safe and economical transportation."

A supporter of Metro communities, Dwyer strongly believes in sharing good fortune. In 1997 he donated five Chrysler mini-vans to community groups to take kids camping. He supports preschool lunch programs throughout the Metro area, as well as numerous other charities.

Metro Halifax has four successful Chrysler dealerships. As Dwyer explains, "I don't need to be the biggest one in terms of numbers or dollars—I just want to be the best retailer by looking after my customers and helping my community prosper."

Joseph T. Flinn and Jane E. Powell of Dartmouth sum up their positive experience at Courtesy Chrysler: "The professional, but personable, manner in which we were dealt with won our business in one night. In short, all our expectations were surpassed. For this we'll be recommending and returning to Courtesy Chrysler." ❖

SHERATON HALIFAX HOTEL

When it comes to location, it would be impossible to find a better place for a first-class hotel than along the shores of bustling Halifax harbour, right in the heart of its historic downtown.

Established in 1985, this unique urban resort is the only hotel located right on the city's beautifully restored harbourfront. Situated in the heart of the famous Historic Properties and surrounded by memories of Halifax's history, colourful shops, lively pubs and fascinating museums await guests right at the Sheraton's doorstep. The harbourfront, with its endless parade of container ships, naval vessels, tugs and pleasure boats, beckons to the right, while up the hill to the left is the renowned Citadel Fortress, just waiting to be explored. The harbourfront and surrounding communities of this dynamic port city are steeped in history and alive with activity. A short drive along the seashore is visually stimulating, and picturesque Peggy's Cove (just 30 kilometres away) offers a glimpse of the traditional Maritime lifestyle and the awesome power of the Atlantic Ocean.

The Sheraton Halifax Hotel's design team, Lydon Lynch Architects Limited of Halifax, won the prestigious Nova Scotia architectural award of excellence for the hotel's innovative design. Inside, guests find an elegant lobby, deluxe guest rooms and a variety of places to wine and dine. In fact, the Sheraton Halifax offers business, convention and leisure travelers superb accommodation and luxurious amenities. Its well-appointed, comfortable and spacious guest rooms are equipped with work desk, computer and fax access, voice mail, in-room coffee and much more. The hotel's newly renovated Club Level floor extends all of the amenities the well traveled business guest has come to expect.

All windows in the deluxe harbour rooms, junior executive and one- and two-bedroom suites open to the fresh sea air and the sound of harbour activities. Other amenities to ensure the comfort and entertainment of guests include an indoor heated swimming pool, a fully equipped health club and a popular licensed rooftop sundeck.

Over 15,000 square feet of modern, flexible, superbly functioning meeting space serves groups of 10 to 800 guests. Every detail, from the initial inquiry to the execution of the program, is handled by dedicated Conference Service Managers, Sheraton One-Stop Managers and professional catering staff. On-site audio and video expertise is provided by I.S.T.S. Telav, making the Sheraton an excellent venue for large conferences and meetings.

For business or pleasure dining, guests can stay inside the front doors of the Sheraton to experience a fine offering of Nova Scotia cuisine. Dine in the elegance of the hotel's main restaurant, or kick back and relax with some real Maritime flavour at The Fife and Drum Pub. Guests who are in a hurry to absorb the history and excitement of Halifax can grab a quick bite at the Edible Express, or take a picnic to enjoy as they roam the city.

Sheraton Halifax Hotel is the only hotel located right on the city's beautifully restored harbourfront.

The Sheraton Halifax Hotel was a major partner in developing the Downtown Halifax Link, a covered overhead pedway which links the best of downtown Halifax together. The Link provides year-round, climate controlled access to 130 boutiques, shops, dining options, banking, parking and entertainment hot spots, including the Sheraton Casino Halifax. As well, the Link assures visitors a safe, clean, walkable city core.

The Downtown Halifax Link and its member hotels offer access to 1,000 guest rooms and over 100,000 square feet of meeting space at the World Trade and Convention Centre. Add the convenience of one-call booking for all facilities, a hassle-free Housing Bureau for conference delegates and other essential services, meetings and conventions are guaranteed to run smoothly. As a member of the City Sell group, the Sheraton Halifax actively participates in joint sales initiatives

For business or pleasure dining, guests can stay inside the front doors of the Sheraton to experience a fine offering of Nova Scotia cuisine (above and left).

with other hospitality partners to attract convention business on a national and international scale by hosting customer events and showcasing Halifax in Ottawa, Toronto and other major areas.

In keeping with Halifax's rich historical background, suites at the Sheraton are named in honor of a few of its local heroes. The Sir Samuel Cunard Suite was named after the founder of Cunard Ship Lines, whose remains rest in Halifax. This luxurious suite features a private dining table for eight, as well as a Jacuzzi, fireplace, grand piano and wet bar. The Sir John Wentworth Suite was named after the first lieutenant governor of Nova Scotia, and the Captain Angus Walter Suite bears the name of the captain of the province's seafaring ambassador, the *Bluenose II* schooner.

Halifax harbour, with its ever-changing vista, laps nearly at your feet, and the beauty and tranquillity reflected there abounds in the Sheraton Halifax Hotel as it extends its hospitality. For business or pleasure or a combination of both, this is where the action is; this is where Halifax shines.

Come, stay and play at the Sheraton Halifax Hotel. ❖

MARANOVA SUITES HOTEL

Maranova Suites Hotel, a stone's throw from Halifax Harbour, boasts a fabulous view of Halifax's waterfront and skyline, delightful by day light and spectacular at night !

Newly renovated, Maranova Suites Hotel in downtown Dartmouth offers comfort, convenience and value, a "Home Away from Home" for many corporate visitors to the Metro area, whether their stay is for a night, a week, or longer. Each room is completely furnished with refrigerator, stove, oven and kitchen utensils, of particular appeal to guests who prefer to dine in. Housekeeping services, air-conditioning, remote control cable television and in-room coffee-makers make the rooms a cozy place to return to at the end of each business day.

The comforts of home are always available at Maranova Suites Hotel. It has licensed restaurant and lounge, coin-operated laundry facilities and convenient underground parking, all maintained with precise attention to detail.

On arrival our guests receive a complimentary 1-day pass to Dartmouth Sportsplex, a full-service athletic complex.

Maranova Suites Hotel is ideally situated within an easy five minute walk to the ferry terminal for a relaxing 15-minute boat ride to the heart of downtown Halifax.

The Hotel offers very competitive rates with first-class service and clean, comfortable accommodations.

Maranova Suites Hotel has single and double rooms, as well as one and two bedroom suites. Penthouse suites with a captivating view of the harbour and Halifax skyline are in high demand with executives. Smoking and non-smoking rooms are also available.

Hotel staff is friendly and knowledgeable and always available to assist. Maranova Suites Hotel is well equipped to meet the business needs of its visitors with fully equipped meeting rooms, photocopy and facsimile services. Flexible billing arrangements are also offered for corporate clients and preferred commercial and government rates.

With all of its amenities, excellent location and competitive rates, it is no wonder Maranova Suites Hotel is a popular and frequent choice for visitors to the "Greater Halifax" area. ⁜

Photo by Jocelin d'Entremont.

Photo by Jocelin d'Entremont.

BIBLIOGRAPHY

Cornwallis, Edward, Letter of June 22, 1949. Public Archives of Nova Scotia MG 100, vol. 126, #18.

Halifax: A Literary Portrait. Edited by John Bell. Pottersfield Press. Lawrencetown Beach, Nova Scotia. 1990.

Jeffers, Alan and Gordon, Rob. *Titanic Halifax, A Guide to Sites*. Nimbus Publishing, Halifax. 1998

Kitz, Janet. *Shattered City: the Halifax Explosion and the Road to Recovery*. Nimbus Publishing, Halifax. 1989

MacNeal, Robert. *Burden of Desire*. Doubleday. New York. 1989.

McLean, Grant. *Walk Historic Halifax*. Nimbus Publishing, Halifax. 1996.

Mitic, Trudy Duivenvoorden, Leblanc, J.P. Pier 21. The Gateway that Changed Canada. Nimbus Publishing. Halifax. 1997.

Nova Scotia Legislative Library catalogue, on line at www.gov.ns.ca.

Raddall, Thomas H. *Governor's Lady*. Doubleday & Company. New York. 1960.

Raddall, Thomas H. *Halifax, Warden of the North*. Doubleday & Company. New York. 1965.

Raddall, Thomas H. *Hangman's Beach*. McClelland and Stewart. 1979

Photo by Jocelin d'Entremont.

ENTERPRISES INDEX

Photo by Julian Beveridge.

141

INDEX

Photo by Jocelin d'Entremont.